WEALTH COMPASS

NAVIGATING THE STOCK MARKET WITHOUT SINKING

FROM COMMUNISTS TO CAPITALISTS:
WHAT BANKS DON'T WANT YOU TO KNOW

BY
JETT QUELLER

DISCLOSURE

We hold 0% in the companies mentioned.

The content of this material is provided for information purposes only and is not advice.

WEALTH COMPASS

Copyright © 2024 by neurodivergent

All rights reserved. No portion of this book may be reproduced, copied, distributed, or adapted in any way, with the exception of certain activities permitted by applicable copyright laws, such as brief quotations in the context of a review or academic work. For permission to publish, distribute or otherwise reproduce this work, please contact the author.

ACKNOWLEDGEMENT

I want to extend my heartfelt gratitude to Sean Peche, Brian Feroldi, Brian Stoffel, and the entire Compounding Quality team for their invaluable inspiration. Their wisdom and insights have been a beacon of knowledge throughout my journey into the financial world.

The images, quotes, and rich content they've shared have enriched this book and shaped the way I think and approach investing. Each concept explained and every piece of advice given has left a lasting imprint on these pages. Thank you for lighting the way and for the profound impact you've made on investors and readers alike.

Your contributions are deeply appreciated and duly recognized.

WHY FROM **COMMUNISTS** TO **CAPITALISTS**?

"Your heart goes on your left, your wallet on your right."

This is what my grandfather used to tell me. Like me, he wasn't a famous thinker, investor, or politician—just a hardworking man who enjoyed traveling and making friends. He was my hero. Inspired by him, I have always been passionate about socializing and learning from everyone, without seeking credit. That's why you won't find information about the author here. But don't worry, I will quote more famous people from now on. As Newton said, "If I have seen further, it is by standing on the shoulders of giants," and this is what I have done—my whole life has been surrounded by giants, learning from them without any complexes.

Learning to invest is not going to turn you into a heartless capitalist machine. Naval Ravikant explained it perfectly in an interview: "Socialism comes from the heart; we all want to be socialists. Capitalism comes from the head. When you're young, if you're not a socialist, you have no heart. But when you're older, if you're not a capitalist, you have no head."

I always appreciate Nassim Taleb's framing of this concept: "With my family, I'm a communist. With my close friends, I'm a socialist. At my state level politics, I'm a democrat. At higher levels, I'm a republican. And at the federal level, I'm a libertarian." This brilliantly captures the idea that our values and governance preferences shift based on context and scale.

The larger the group of people with different interests, the less trust there is, and the more aligned the incentives need to be. Thus, the better the system has to work, the more you lean towards capitalism. Conversely, in smaller, more intimate groups like your family or close friends, socialism thrives. It's about living a loving, happy, integrated life within your tribe. But applying socialism on a larger scale is impractical. As Taleb humorously implies, if you want to be a real socialist, open all your doors and windows tomorrow and let everyone take what they want—see how that works out. Unfortunately, human nature is the best argument against socialism.

If you wonder why all this political stuff is in an investment book, keep reading. You will see that to invest you won't only need your head but your heart, and most importantly, your gut.

In a world filled with financial distractions and quick-profit schemes, discovering the path to true investment success may seem like a challenging journey. However, fear not – we're here to provide guidance and support. Get ready for an exciting exploration of the stock market, led by a reliable source that prioritizes simplicity over complexity. Unlocking Investment Success goes beyond the typical investment guide; it offers a thorough yet accessible journey through the complexities of stock investing.

↗ Your Trusted Guide

We won't hand you a one-size-fits-all guide or guarantee shortcuts to success. Instead, we'll use our knowledge, experience and expertise to equip you. From the foundational principles of stocks to the intricacies of compounding, from valuation strategies to the practices of seasoned investors – we cover it all. Myths? Consider them busted.

↗ A Companion in the World of Investment

In a world saturated with flashy trends and 'hot tips', we remain committed to the fundamental principles that drive success in investing. We know that genuine wealth isn't about fleeting gains but about gradual, steady growth. Our mission is to empower you with knowledge so that your investment choices resonate with your financial ambitions, risk tolerance, and time frame.

↗ Restful Sleep and Financial Security

Let's be real – anyone promising instant wealth is just blowing smoke. What we offer is far more valuable – keys to understanding and navigating the intricacies of the investment realm. We may not guarantee sky-high returns, but we assure you the peace of mind that stems from well-informed decisions. Rest assured that the majority of our own funds are invested exactly as we recommend. We rest easy at night and so can you, knowing your hard-earned money is working diligently on your behalf even while you sleep.

↗ The Book They'd Rather You Didn't Possess

This isn't the kind of book that financial titans want you to grace your shelves with. Nor is it one that adherents of communism would openly share they're reading. This is for you – the individual, the seeker of financial wisdom, the conscious investor. We've deciphered the complexities and demystified the jargon, ensuring that anyone can grasp the concepts that steer the financial realm.

↗ An Invitation to Empowerment and Growth

Investing wisely isn't about blind obedience to trends or chasing fleeting wins. It's about fostering having the courage to stand by your decisions while being open to recalibrations when necessary. From these pages, you'll accumulate insights and deep financial wisdom. Armed with these, you'll stride confidently into the ever-evolving arena of the stock market, poised to make decisions that mirror your values, dreams, and aspirations.

Anyone can **learn** to **invest** and we're here to **teach you**.
Welcome.

DISCLAIMER

'Investing is **simple** but not **easy**.'
— Warren Buffet

This book is not intended to serve as financial advice. As Peter Lynch insightfully pointed out, 'Everyone has the brain power to make money in stocks. Not everyone has the stomach.'

This book is my personal financial bible which guides me to stay the course and trust that, in the long run, the market tends to reward the patient and disciplined. It restores my faith when needed.

Amidst the flurry of complex terminology from Wall Street, which often serves more to dazzle than educate, I aim to provide clear guidance and information to bolster your confidence during the market's inevitable swings. It's true — the market often appears more irrational than not, but ultimately, I believe it gives each investor what they've truly earned.

Real-world examples can shed light on the market's inner workings, yet they might not always prevent the need to reread a passage or seek out explanations from trusty resources like Google or contemporary tools like ChatGPT. If grappling with challenging concepts in the text makes you uncomfortable, you might also find the volatility of investing challenging.

In today's world, where investing is more accessible than ever, market fluctuations are common as investors tend to hold onto stocks for shorter periods. Embrace the paradox of our times. For instance, the abundance of information at our fingertips, while making research effortless, also contributes to increased market volatility. This makes the whole investing thing scary. This same volatility, however, presents us with the advantage of buying quality stocks at attractive prices.

In this book, by utilizing everyday examples, I hope to demystify the mechanics of the market. Nonetheless, be prepared to revisit some sections, consult with Saint Google, or even chat with AI assistants like ChatGPT. Investment requires endurance, not just of intellect but of nerve. If the thought of your investments tumbling by 20% makes you uneasy, then the world of investing might not be your playground.

Remember though, volatility isn't synonymous with risk—it simply adds colour to the investor's journey and can present greater opportunities to those who are willing to endure the downsides without knowing their duration. To understand investing, imagine riding a bicycle around your neighbourhood: the route you choose dictates the intensity of the ride. In the financial world, what feels like an uphill battle can lead to the rewarding glide downhill—though, in the market, the ups and downs feelings are switched.

See this book through and your perseverance will be rewarded not only in these pages but also in the market and your chosen investments. Embrace the complex sections, feed your inquisitiveness, and you'll discover how to delve deeper into the history and fundamentals of stocks. By engaging with the material, highlighting important insights, and supplementing your knowledge, you'll grow to understand and love the ebb and flow of the market. Care for your investments, weed out the unproductive ones, and watch your financial garden thrive.

Let's start this journey—an odyssey of numbers, strategy, and the pursuit of financial growth.

A NOTE ON
REPETITION AND MINDSET

Before diving deeper into this book, I'd like to address a particular characteristic of its content. As Peter Lynch, one of the greats in the investing world, wisely remarked, 'Everyone has the brain power to make money in stocks, not everyone has the stomach.' This statement, while simple, speaks volumes about the duality of intelligence and emotional resilience required in the world of investing.

This book may not be the kind you revisit time and again, like those timeless masterpieces that offer fresh insights with every reading. Some concepts might be reiterated in various sections. This repetition isn't an oversight or redundancy. Instead, it's a deliberate effort to engrain certain pivotal principles, presenting them in different lights and contexts so they settle firmly in your understanding.

Acquiring an investor's mindset isn't just about rote learning or memorization. It's about cultivating a habit and developing an instinctive response mechanism. It's about training both the brain and the gut. Investing often requires one to stand firm in the face of market volatility, to hold one's nerve when others are panicking, and to possess the courage of one's convictions. As such, some principles bear repeating, to fortify your intellectual understanding and emotional resilience alike.

So, as you make your way through these pages, embrace the repetition. See it as a reinforcement of the pillars of investing wisdom. Remember, in the world of stocks and investments, success is often more about having a resilient gut than a sharp brain.

CONTENTS

Acknowledgement 5

Introduction 19

Chapter 1
Investing and Financial Freedom 24

Chapter 2
Economic Cycles and Financial Markets 40

Chapter 3
Active Investing vs. Passive Investing 52

Chapter 4
The Conservative Investor and Common Stock –
General Rules for Investing 66

Chapter 5
Financial Metrics to Gauge Company's
Financial Strength 84

Chapter 6
Corporate Governance Practices -
Why Are They Important for Investing? 126

Chapter 7
Two Important Approaches to Investing –
Growth and Value Investing 164

Chapter 8
Decoding the Compounding Power for Creating Wealth ... 186

Chapter 9
Building a Portfolio with Optimal Portfolio Diversification ... 208

Chapter 10
The Final Verdict – Unraveling the Investing Paradox 228

Bonus Chapter
A Few Important Company Case Histories and
Quotes from Legend 132

INTRODUCTION

You're probably familiar with the age-old concept of 'making money while you sleep'. However, what if we told you that it's time to flip that narrative? Welcome to the world of 'making sleep while making money'. Yes, you read that right. Our focus here isn't just about accumulating wealth; it's also about ensuring that your nights are peaceful because investing without understanding is the surest recipe for those dreaded sleepless nights.

In the chapters that follow, we'll dive into intriguing territories, where financial wisdom meets engaging narratives. Brace yourself for an exploration of ideas that might sound downright bananas at first glance. Have you ever heard the one about the monkeys that outperformed seasoned investors in portfolio management? It might seem like the start of a joke, but the lesson behind this peculiar tale is priceless. Then, there's the curious link between successful investing and sociopathic traits. Odd, right? Yet, stick with us, and we'll untangle these mysteries together, presenting insights and practical lessons that can transform your finances.

Because we don't want you to go through the entire book just to tell you to buy an index fund. We are value investors, so we aim not only to teach you where to find them but also to deliver value through this book.

As we look at the various investing strategies, we aim to arm you with knowledge and understanding. This newfound wisdom will help you approach investing with confidence and attain that blissful state where financial decisions don't steal your sleep.

So, how do we achieve this? We need to dive into the market, understand it, and even grow to love it. We'll start right here with understanding stocks. They're more than just pieces of paper; they are a slice of the very businesses that drive our world. When you invest in a company's stock, you're not just buying digits on a screen; you're becoming a part-owner of that enterprise.

Knowing this should help you to think like an owner, not a trader. While the allure of trendy, skyrocketing stocks can be hard to resist, it's crucial to pause and ponder before buying them. What are you truly gaining when you invest in a company's stock? It's not just a virtual number; it's an actual stake in a thriving, operational business.

This shift in perspective can revolutionize your entire approach to investing. Just as the Oracle of Omaha, Warren Buffett, elegantly puts it: 'Price is what you pay, value is what you get.' It's not about chasing trends; it's about discerning the inherent value of the company you're investing in.

Investing isn't a guessing game; it's a journey of well-calculated decisions grounded in a company's genuine worth. By thinking like an owner, you're more likely to make strategic, long-term investments that yield substantial returns over time.

Allow us to borrow a famous Chinese proverb: 'The best time to plant a tree was 20 years ago. The second-best time is now.' This holds true for investing. While it would have been fantastic to start investing years ago, the next best moment is this very instant. Don't worry, even if you're new to this, armed with a little knowledge, even a beginner can make informed investment decisions.

Introduction

Welcome to the captivating world of investing, where the allure of instant gains often takes centre stage. It's a realm where the crowd cheers for the soaring stars – those stocks that grab headlines and set pulses racing. However, as value investors, we know there's a different route to enduring success – one that involves falling in love with stocks that possess timeless qualities and the potential for lasting partnerships.

Imagine a high school scenario where the popular kids bask in adoration, flaunting confidence and charisma. They seem to have it all figured out. They're the essence of a thrilling future. Yet, time reveals the cracks beneath their glamorous facade – multiple divorces, struggles with addiction, and personal demons. On the other hand, there's the quiet observer, a student diligently building a strong foundation for the future, away from the spotlight. As the years roll by, this unassuming individual emerges as the true victor, having found genuine happiness and fulfilment.

In the investment realm, we aim to pinpoint these quiet achievers – the stocks that might not make headlines but have the potential for steady growth. We're in search of companies with robust fundamentals, reliable management, and the promise of sustained progress over time. These are the stocks that can accompany us on the journey to wealth creation, adding value to our lives just like long-term partners.

'Falling in love with stocks' isn't just a catchy phrase; it's a mindset. It's about forging deep relationships with the companies we invest in, just like we do with people in our personal lives. Genuine affection demands understanding, trust, and the readiness to weather challenges. It's about embracing a long-term perspective and resisting the temptation of short-term market fluctuations.

Dear reader, get ready to delve into the exciting realm of investing. We're here to equip you with the tools and insights that will shed light on the world of investing and enhance your financial path. Let's challenge conventional thinking, prioritize enduring qualities, and view our investments as long-term allies in our pursuit of prosperity.

As we venture into the captivating world of investing, it's essential to ask, 'Why invest in the stock market when there are seemingly simpler options like real estate?' This book aims to address this question and lay the groundwork for a thorough understanding of the stock market.

Are you prepared to explore the dynamic world of stock market investing? Let's begin!

CHAPTER 1

INVESTING AND FINANCIAL FREEDOM

Investing is not just about numbers on a chart or the glint of gold coins; it's about a pursuit. In a world where the only constant is change, investing becomes the anchor that can help secure your financial future.

↗ Stocks vs. Real Estate: A Comparative Analysis

Most people understand the concept of investing in real estate: you buy a property, rent it out, and collect a monthly income. But when it comes to investing in the stock market, many are hesitant. It's important, however, to understand that stocks can provide similar, if not better, benefits than real estate.

Like real estate, established companies' stocks offer regular income through dividends. Moreover, the potential for price appreciation in stocks can be compared to buying a piece of land and waiting for its value to increase.

At a glance, real estate might seem like the safer bet for many. It's tangible; you can see and touch it. It's an asset that, historically, has been associated with wealth creation. However, in today's fast-paced world, the stock market has proven to be a worthy adversary to this traditional investment channel. Here are a few reasons why.

1. Accessibility and Initial Investment

Purchasing real estate typically requires a substantial initial capital outlay. This is often amplified by additional costs like high-interest loans. In certain countries, when you acquire property and thereby increase your asset value, there's an added tax implication. Governments in these regions impose capital gains taxes, which can be as much as 10% of the property's value. This taxation is effectively penalizing you for augmenting your equity.

To put this into perspective, imagine if you were to pay a 10% management fee for your stock investments. Such a fee would be exorbitant, especially when compared to the typical management fees for stocks, which generally range from 0.25% to 4%. A fee below 1.25% is considered reasonable by many, contingent upon the array of services provided by the manager.

In contrast, stocks are far more accessible. For the price of a down payment on a property, one could diversify across various stocks, spreading risk and potentially enhancing returns.

While stocks are more accessible, it's still essential to be well-informed before diving in. It's the knowledge barrier, not just the capital barrier that prevents many from venturing into stocks. Addressing this knowledge barrier is one of this book's primary goals. We want to empower readers with the insights and understanding they need to confidently navigate the world of stocks.

2. **Liquidity**

Properties aren't easy to sell. Selling involves paperwork, time, and often, additional costs. Stocks, on the other hand, provide liquidity. A well-selected portfolio can be turned into cash in mere moments, proving invaluable during unforeseen financial challenges.

3. **Income Potential**

Much like a rented property provides monthly income, stocks of established companies offer dividends – a regular income stream for investors. Furthermore, as the company grows, so does the potential for stock appreciation, akin to the land's value rising over time.

4. Diversification and Risk Management

Real estate investments often tie up a large portion of one's capital in a single asset. Stocks allow for diversification. A dip in one company's fortunes can be offset by the rise of another in your portfolio. While both have their risks — stocks can be volatile and properties can remain vacant or depreciate — diversification across various assets is the key to risk mitigation.

5. The True Value Perspective

One of the common pitfalls for novice investors in the stock market is the confusion between price and value. Prices fluctuate, sometimes wildly, influenced by a myriad of factors ranging from economic indicators to geopolitical events. However, a company's inherent value — its assets, earnings potential and management quality — tends to be far more stable.

It's this distinction that seasoned investors leverage. While the impatient may panic and sell during a market dip, those focused on true value see opportunities. They understand that frequent transactions often benefit only the intermediaries — banks, brokers, and other financial institutions. Their profits rise with transaction frequency, but astute investors prioritize a longer horizon, focusing on genuine value and potential.

↗ Why We Need to Invest

You must have often heard people saying, 'He just got lucky' when they see someone turn a startup into a $1 billion company or when an entrepreneur grows his business empire significantly to worth $100 billion.

So, were they just lucky, or did they do something different? It would be right to put it this way – They were at the right place at the right time and they knew the art of creating wealth. You must have heard of people like Bill Gates, Steve Jobs, Warren Buffett, and many others like them who have created a large fortune. Now, if one said that they just 'got lucky', this would be quite unfair. It would ignore the fact that they made it big in life because of their incredible knowledge and investment of that knowledge into the right businesses. This helped them compound their wealth over time.

Earning a good amount of money is just not enough. Our life is influenced by many factors even though we may believe that we have control over it. It is influenced by the environment we live in, the economic conditions of our country and around the world, and geopolitics which indirectly impacts the lives of the common people. Just think of people who lost everything during the Great Depression of the 1930s or the 2008 Financial Crisis, the most severe global economic crisis since the Great Depression, which exposed the failures of the global financial system. Not to mention the COVID-19 pandemic that brought the entire world to a standstill.

These global economic crises impacted the lives of common people in many ways. Many lost their jobs while others struggled to run their businesses and were forced to shut down. Thus, it becomes indispensable to not only save money during our good times but also make that money grow to help us when we need it the most. This is why investing is necessary.

In simple terms, investing can be defined as a **commitment of money toward buying an asset to generate income payments or capital gains.** Thus, you can **understand investing as a**

means of growing money over time. There is a wide spectrum of assets in which one can invest money to earn a return over time. Each asset class is a group of financial instruments that exhibit certain characteristics specific to that group. Some examples of asset classes are fixed-income instruments, bonds, equities, commodities, real estate, digital assets, and even fine arts and antiques. Each asset class has its own risk. and the most popular asset class among the common people is stocks or equities.

A stock or equity investment represents fractional ownership in that business. Thus, individuals invest in stocks hoping that the company will grow over time, and, in turn, the value of their shares will increase.

Historical Background

Investing can find its roots in the 17th and 18th centuries when the first public markets, such as the Amsterdam Stock Exchange, established in 1602, and the New York Stock Exchange (NYSE) in 1792, enabled investors with investment opportunities.

The Industrial Revolutions during the 18th and early 19th centuries brought greater prosperity, enabling people to amass savings that could be invested in developing the advanced financial banking system.

The 20th century saw investment concepts like asset pricing and portfolio theory developments. In the second half of the century, new investment vehicles, such as private equity, venture capital, REITs and so on came into the picture. Finally, with the development of the Internet in the 1990s, online trading, and investment opportunities became more easily accessible to the general public, which led to the democratization of investing.

The recent notable financial events of the 21st century include the dot-com bubble, the 2008 global financial crisis, and the 2020 global COVID pandemic.

↗ Understanding Basic Money Concepts

Let's first understand the concepts of money, purchasing power, and inflation before looking deeper into why investing is necessary.

The art of investing has long been interwoven with the fabric of human civilization. While we might associate modern stock markets with sprawling cities, the history stretches far beyond these contemporary urban landscapes.

In the early 17th century, Amsterdam was a bustling hub of trade and finance. Amidst this was a merchant, Isaac Le Maire, who had ambition and foresight. Le Maire is a fascinating figure in the annals of investing. Not only did he recognize the vast potential of shares in the Dutch East India Company, the world's first publicly traded company, but he also became one of the first individuals to engage in 'short selling'. Betting against the general sentiment, he audaciously sold shares he didn't own, hoping to buy them back at a lower price. His gambit, whether successful or not, showcased the beginnings of strategies that would later become common in the vast arenas of Wall Street.

Fast forward to the streets of New York in 1792. Before the grand New York Stock Exchange (NYSE) came into existence, a modest buttonwood tree on Wall Street played host to merchants and stockbrokers. They gathered beneath its branches, trading informally and shaping the future of the financial world. Recognizing the need for a more structured approach, these early pioneers signed the Buttonwood Agreement. This simple yet groundbreaking document paved the way for the establishment of the NYSE. What began under the shade of a tree would soon become the centre of global finance.

These tales show the passion, foresight, and audacity that shaped the world of investing. They remind us that behind every ticker symbol and stock index, there's a story waiting to be told.

↗ The Silent Thief: Eroding Purchasing Power

Money, as you know, is a medium of exchange for purchasing various goods and services, and purchasing power is the amount of those goods and services that can be purchased with one unit of currency.

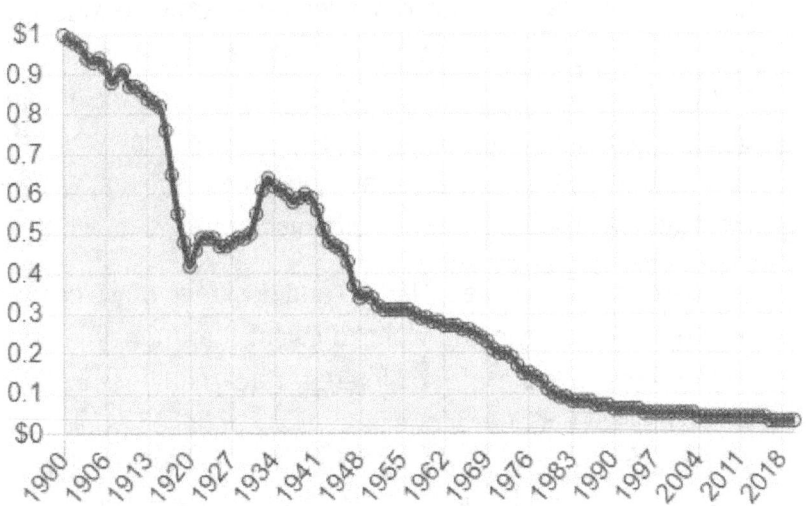

BUYING POWER OF $1 OVER TIME, 1900-2020

Source: https://twitter.com/qcompounding/status/1669720226831691778

Inflation, on the other hand, means a reduction in the purchasing power of money with an increase in the prices of goods and services. Now, we can correlate these terms to understand why investing is necessary through an example.

To truly grasp the concept of purchasing power, let's undertake an elementary, yet profoundly telling exercise. Consider the quintessential fast-food item known globally - the Big Mac. Its price has changed over the years, reflecting not just the costs of ingredients or labour, but also the decreasing value of the dollar. Let's take a closer look.

Year	Minimum Wage (USD/Hour)	Big Mac Price (USD)	Burgers per Hour Worked
1980	$3.10	$1.60	1.94
2022	$7.25	$5.81	1.25

In 1980, a person earning the minimum wage could buy about 6.20 Big Macs with an hour's earnings. Fast forward to 2022, and that same person could buy less than one Big Mac with an hour's wage. This isn't merely an observation about the rising cost of burgers; it's a poignant reflection on the erosion of purchasing power over time. This means that while the numbers on your pay check may have grown, the real value – what you can buy with it – has diminished.

Suppose you have saved $15,000 and decide to buy a car, not now but after a year, and want to invest that money in bond instruments offering a 3.4% interest rate yearly. Hence, you would have $15,510 after one year. Also, car prices would have increased by 3.5% due to inflation during that one year. Now, when you want to buy, the same car would cost $15,525 due to inflation. This shows that investing in bonds for a year wasn't enough to cover the car's cost, let alone generate additional cash for savings.

On the other hand, suppose you had invested in an S&P 500 index which has generated a 9.27% average annual return for the past five years from 2018 to 2022. In that case, even taking an 8% return after discounting for inflation, taxes, and other costs, you would still be left with $16,200 after a year, which would have easily covered your car cost of $15,525 and left you additional cash of $675.

Now you know why investing is necessary to beat inflation and generate additional returns that can help compound wealth. You'll now be able to identify with these words of investor Peter Lynch: 'If you invest $1,000 in a stock, all you can lose is $1,000, but you stand to gain $10,000 or even $50,000 over time if you're patient.'

The Widening Chasm:
The Rich Get Richer, The Poor Get Poorer

As we journey further into the financial realm, it becomes evident that there's a growing disparity between the affluent and the less privileged. The rich, with their vast resources and access to information, have tools to hedge against this erosion of purchasing power. They invest in assets like stocks, real estate, and businesses that appreciate over time, effectively shielding their wealth from inflation.

The less privileged, often caught in the trap of living from pay check to pay check, find it challenging to invest and protect their wealth. As a result, their money loses value faster than they can earn it. This disparity is an age-old conundrum. The rich leverage their resources to accumulate more wealth while the poor remain ensnared in a cycle of financial stagnation.

Some might argue that a cataclysmic event, like an apocalypse or human extinction, would level this playing field. In such a scenario, stocks might plummet, and cash may lose all value. But that's an extreme perspective. The truth is, there are ways to break this cycle and to empower individuals with knowledge and tools that can pave the path to financial freedom.

Stephen Hawking, the renowned physicist, reduced his expectations to zero when he was diagnosed with Lou Gehrig's disease at the age of 21. Everything for him after that was a bonus. If you start investing now, then adopting a pessimistic plan can be beneficial for you. This approach will allow you to secure your elderly years and leave behind financial support for your loved ones. A pessimistic plan can leave you pleasantly surprised and bring optimistic outcomes when your returns outperform your expectations, leaving your life sorted even before you expected it and allowing you ample time to spend with your loved ones.

Of course, investing in any stock or equity does not guarantee sure-shot returns, and there are various reasons for this. For example, an equity index fund may rise over time, but it does not necessarily mean all the stocks constituting it would have risen in tandem with the index. However, it could be because the company would have performed badly over the period, so its stock would have fallen.

The below graph of the S&P 500 indicates how the index has performed over the last 100 years. The grey vertical lines indicate periods of recession where the index performed negatively for the short intermittent periods but produced tremendous returns over the long run.

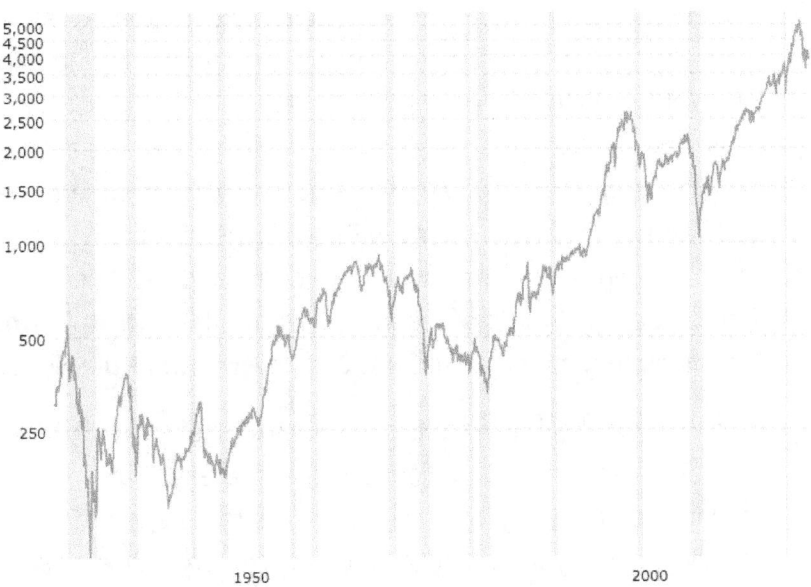

Source: https://www.macrotrends.net/2324/sp-500-historical-chart-data

After seeing the graph, you may be excited and ready to start investing immediately! Investing can certainly be an exciting and rewarding way to grow your wealth, but it's important to approach it with caution and knowledge. With so many investment opportunities available, it can be tempting to jump in headfirst without fully understanding what you're investing in. This can be a recipe for sleepless nights and financial disaster.

Investing without understanding can lead to several negative outcomes, including losing your hard-earned money, feeling anxious or stressed about your investments, and experiencing a negative impact on your mental health. To avoid these outcomes, it's important to take the time to research and understand what you're investing in.

One common mistake that people make when investing is chasing after the latest trend or hot stock without fully understanding the underlying fundamentals of the investment. This can lead to poor investment decisions and can even result in significant losses. It's important to understand the risks and rewards associated with any investment and to only invest in things that align with your goals and risk tolerance. Remember the words of legendary Warren Buffett, **'Rule No. 1 is never lose money. Rule No. 2 is never forget Rule No. 1.'**

Another mistake that investors often make is failing to diversify their investments. Diversification is a strategy that involves investing in a variety of different assets to spread your risk. By diversifying your portfolio, you can reduce your exposure to any one investment and increase your chances of earning a positive return. Failing to diversify can leave you vulnerable to market downturns and other unexpected events that could negatively impact your investments.

Financial Freedom and Enlightened Investing

What does financial freedom mean to you? Do you see it as sipping cocktails on a beach? Perhaps, but it's deeper than that. True financial freedom is not about continuous leisure, but rather the luxury of working on your terms. It means working because you're passionate and inspired, not because bills are due. You might have noticed that those idyllic vacation spots aren't always overflowing with millionaires, at least not year-round.

Investing, when understood, is an art. It demands patience, strategy, and an unwavering belief in the process. This is where many falter. People are often eager to invest, but not as keen on learning the art of investment. Yet, the best investment anyone can make is in themselves—through acquiring knowledge. The difference between successful investors and those facing financial calamities often boils down to education and mindset. Once you realize that cash, especially cash lying idly in banks, essentially depreciates, your perspective shifts. Money in the bank can sometimes be equivalent to having no money at all when factoring in inflation and other economic variables. This realization propels many to save diligently, not just for the sake of hoarding, but to actively seek growth opportunities like stocks, giving purpose to their savings.

However, before one ventures into investing, it's essential to have a clear picture of their financial health. Basic financial literacy—understanding your expenses versus income, knowing your liabilities, being aware of pending credits, and ensuring you always maintain an emergency fund—is pivotal. **Your income should invariably exceed your expenses. That's the golden rule.** If ever there's an unforeseen circumstance leading to a reduction in income, it's that savings buffer that will keep you afloat.

Investing without a solid understanding can be detrimental to your financial well-being and your mental health. Financial worries are significant anxiety triggers, leading to physical and emotional strain. But the good news? You can safeguard against this. Investing in understanding your investments, their risks, rewards, and intricacies can significantly alleviate such stresses. Don't just throw money into stocks or assets; know why you're doing it and have a strategy in place.

We want to break down these complexities for you and transform hesitant savers into enlightened investors. Whether your goal is to build a retirement nest egg or finance your child's future education, this guide will equip you with the tools and knowledge you need. After all, true financial freedom is not just having money, but understanding how to make that money work effortlessly for you.

↗ The Hope Ahead

While the challenges are real, investing is about hope and confidence. By understanding the dynamics and arming ourselves with the right strategies, we can withstand financial challenges and have a prosperous future.

As we venture further, we'll dissect the stock market intricacies, helping you distinguish between ephemeral price movements and enduring value. We'll introduce you to the different types of stocks, and the importance of corporate governance, and teach you how to assess a company's genuine worth. For it all, we'll use real-world examples and in-depth analyses.

Remember: every master was once a beginner. Every Warren Buffett or Ray Dalio began with a single step, a single investment. And with every chapter of this book, you'll move closer to mastering the art and science of investing. Stay with us as we illuminate the path towards true financial freedom.

CHAPTER 2
ECONOMIC CYCLES AND FINANCIAL MARKETS

'It's not about timing the market, but time in the market that matters.'

– Ann Wilson.

Have you ever made an investment decision based on your assessment of the current stage of the economic cycle? How did it turn out, and what did you learn from that experience? As a beginner, you must first understand the economy to learn how economic cycles influence the financial markets. An economy can be defined as a measure of all activities related to the consumption, production, and trade of goods and services of a region, state or country. In contrast, the stock market is a measure of the financial strength of publicly listed companies.

The economic cycles and the financial markets are closely related. The economic cycles represent expansion and contraction in the overall economic activity. **Each economic cycle consists of four stages: expansion, peak, contraction and trough, and then** the cycle repeats.

Factors such as gross domestic product (GDP), employment rates, and consumer spending determine the ongoing stage of the economic cycle. The GDP used as a measure to determine a country's economy is the total market value of all the goods and services produced in a specific period within the country.

The expansion stage of the economy sees rapid growth as production increases due to low interest rates. As a result, economic activity indicators such as wages, consumer spending, employment rates and corporate profits tend to show an uptrend. Money is cheap due to low interest rates, and the flow of money into the economy keeps it in expansion mode. As companies make higher profits, investors start to show more confidence in them and the same is reflected in the stock prices, which soar due to rising demand. The rising stock market trend is referred to as a 'bull market'.

The expansion phase of the economy reaches a point where growth peaks and economic indicators stabilize. This stage is known as the peak phase. However, continuously rising prices create an economic imbalance, leading to overheated inflation that requires correction. To control inflation, the central bank steps in and increases interest rates, making money more expensive. As a result, consumer spending and demand decrease, leading to lower profits and potential employee layoffs, which, in turn, increases unemployment rates. This phase marks a contraction in economic activity.

Once inflation is under control, interest rates may decrease again, signalling a potential shift in the economic cycle.

As the economy peaks, the rising stock prices also tend to stabilize. Finally, the economic contraction phase makes the stock prices fall as the investors realize a contraction in business activities. Falling stock prices in the stock market by over 20% is known as a 'bear market'. However, the economy finally reaches a low point, with demand and supply levels indicating that economic activity has stopped declining further. Moreover, the economy's low point provides businesses an opportunity to reconfigure their finances with an expectation of economic recovery. As a result, the stock prices and the market, realizing the trough phase of the economy, stop declining further and bottom out.

Value investors start to jump in to accumulate good quality stocks in anticipation of an economic recovery. This completes the economic cycle with four stages, and a new economic cycle repeats. In every economic cycle, opportunities to find value exist, but it becomes easier during recessions when fear dominates the market, leading to undervalued stocks. On the other hand, during the expansion stage, greed can drive many stocks to become overvalued, causing people to overpay. The key is to avoid overpaying for assets and stay vigilant in seeking opportunities based on their intrinsic value.

The economic cycles and the financial markets are closely related to each other. To put it in the words of Robert Shiller, 'The stock market is like a thermometer in a hospital, measuring the health of the economy.' Therefore, as an investor, it is important to understand how the financial markets operate and what influences stock prices. For example, the 2008 financial crisis, also known as the global economic crisis, caused a prolonged economic downturn which led to a fall in stock prices. As a result, the S&P 500 index fell by around 46% in 18 months, from October 2007 to March 2009. The crisis resulted in job losses and reduced consumer spending, leading to a significant economic decline. The governments and central banks of the respective countries stepped in to bail out the troubled financial system and took regulatory measures to stabilize the economy. As the economy started to recover and expand, the prices of the stocks rose, and the S&P 500 regained all its losses by March 2013.

The 2020 COVID-19 pandemic created instability and the stock markets crashed, with stock prices experiencing freefall. The S&P 500 index fell around 36% from its peak. Economic activity was severely affected and declined considerably before beginning to pick up again. As the economy improved, the index rose and touched the 4,000 mark for the first time in April 2021. The graph below shows the relationship between the economy and the stock market. The S&P 500 index, which consists of 500 large companies, is more or less related to the overall economy measured in terms of GDP.

Source: https://fred.stlouisfed.org/series/GDP

↗ Navigating Economic Cycles: Stock Selection and Leading Indicators

Understanding economic cycles is crucial for investors, as it allows them to make informed decisions on which stocks to pick at different stages of the cycle. As we said before, each economic cycle has four stages: expansion, peak, contraction, and trough. Not all stocks perform equally during these stages, so investors must adjust their strategies accordingly. In addition, leading indicators can provide valuable insights into the economy's direction, helping investors to make timely decisions. The words of Seth Klarman best sum it up: 'The stock market is the story of cycles and human behaviour responsible for overreactions in both directions.'

1. **Expansion:** During the expansion stage, economic activity is growing, and corporate profits are on the rise. Investors should consider stocks in cyclical sectors, such as consumer discretionary, industrials and technology. These sectors typically benefit from increased consumer spending, business investment, and overall economic growth.

2. **Peak:** As the economy reaches its peak, growth rates begin to stabilize, and inflationary pressures mount. Investors may

want to shift their focus towards defensive sectors, such as consumer staples, healthcare and utilities. These sectors are less sensitive to economic fluctuations and can provide more stable returns during uncertain times.

3. **Contraction:** During the contraction phase, economic activity declines, and corporate profits may suffer. Investors should prioritize high-quality, dividend-paying stocks in defensive sectors. These companies have a proven track record of weathering economic downturns and can provide a steady stream of income.

4. **Trough:** As the economy bottoms out, investors can start to look for opportunities in cyclical sectors again, as these are likely to benefit from the ensuing economic recovery. Value investors should seek out undervalued companies with strong fundamentals, as these stocks have the potential to deliver significant returns as the economy rebounds.

Now, you must be thinking, 'Are there any sources or tools that you can utilize to monitor economic indicators and market trends?' Certainly, yes! Various essential tools known as leading indicators can help predict changes in economic conditions before they occur. These indicators often move ahead of the overall economy, providing valuable insights into future trends. Some examples of leading indicators include:

1. **Stock Market Indices:** Stock markets often anticipate changes in the economy as investors adjust their expectations based on economic data, corporate earnings and other factors. An upward trend in stock market indices may signal an impending economic expansion, while a downward trend could indicate a coming contraction.

2. **Manufacturing and Services Purchasing Managers' Index (PMI):** The PMI is a survey of purchasing managers in the manufacturing and services sectors, which measures business activity and sentiment. A PMI reading above 50 indicates expansion, while a reading below 50 suggests contraction. Rising PMI levels can signal an impending economic recovery, while falling levels may indicate a slowdown.

3. **Housing Starts:** Housing starts represent the number of new residential construction projects begun during a specific period. An increase in housing starts can signal an upturn in the economy, as it indicates growing consumer confidence and increased demand for homes.

4. **Yield Curve:** The yield curve plots the interest rates of bonds with different maturity dates. A steep yield curve, with long-term rates significantly higher than short-term rates, indicates that investors expect economic growth and inflation in the future. An inverted yield curve, where short-term rates are higher than long-term rates, is often seen as a warning sign of a potential recession.

By monitoring these leading indicators and adjusting their stock selection strategies according to the economic cycle, investors can better position themselves to profit from changing market conditions. It is essential to stay informed and adapt to the shifting economic landscape to maximize investment returns and minimize risk.

The dance between economic cycles and financial markets is a captivating one. Understanding this intricate tango can give you insight into where the market might be headed next. Imagine the stock market as a giant seesaw, balancing on the principles of demand and supply. Sometimes, stocks soar too high, ignoring the reality of their fundamentals and the broader economy. When this happens, gravity (or market corrections) ensures they come back down to earth.

Before leaping into the world of stocks, pause. Assess the market's pulse. This insight can help shield you from overpriced stocks while spotlighting gems available at a discount.

Seasoned investors are akin to market whisperers. They pick up on signals, hints and subtle nudges that hint at upcoming economic shifts. This is because markets are like clairvoyants, gazing roughly six months into the future. Hence the saying, 'The market discounts everything.' This means that any titbit of information that could sway a stock's value is already baked into its price.

However, here's where I want to drop a plot twist into our narrative. Forget everything I just said. Yes, you heard that right! Wipe your mental slate clean and imprint this instead: 'It's not about timing the market, but time in the market that matters.' - Ann Wilson. The prophecy of predicting market movements is a tantalizing game, yet it's riddled with uncertainties. Even if you do guess right, there's the added challenge of forecasting the market's reaction.

'Why did you delve into all that information about economic cycles earlier?' you might wonder. In his book The Most Important Thing, Howard Marks introduces a concept called 'second-level thinking'. Understanding economic cycles can provide insights into when an asset might be overvalued. While many investors try to adjust their assets in anticipation of the coming cycle, with this knowledge, you can secure and retain assets that others may be selling at a discount, ensuring you don't overpay.

Sure, if you have spare hours, indulge in this pastime. But in my time? I won't spend a single minute on divining the future. Let's keep it plain and simple: think long-term. Look at these graphs, and all will be revealed.

In the vast landscape of financial research, few works offer as profound an insight into the historical performance of stocks and bonds as Jeremy Siegel's Stocks for the Long Run. Drawing from this masterpiece, the figure below provides a visual journey spanning over two centuries, contrasting the real returns of stocks against bonds. Siegel's meticulous research underscores a pivotal message for investors: the undeniable potency of equities in long-term wealth generation. Let's delve into this illustrative breakdown to better grasp the evolution of financial markets from 1802 to 2012.

Stocks for the Long Run, 1802-2012

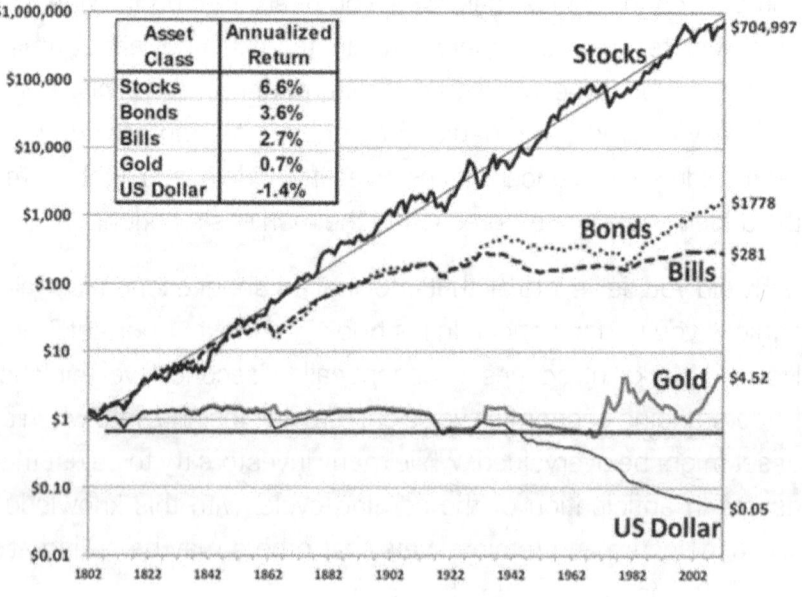

FIGURE 1-1

Total Real Returns on U.S. Stocks, Bonds, Bills, Gold, and the Dollar, 1802–2012

Source: Siegel (2014)
Do Stocks Always Outperform Bonds? — Verdad (verdadcap.com)

'Deciphering the ebbs and flows of the stock market can be a daunting task, yet historical data offers a beacon of clarity. The chart below dives deep into the S&P 500 Index's day-to-day performance since 1942, shedding light on the dynamics of U.S. bull and bear markets over the decades. By revisiting these pivotal cycles of market expansions and recessions, we can draw meaningful insights that emphasize the merits of long-term investing.

- Bull markets, on average, spanned 4.4 years, delivering an impressive cumulative return of 155.7%.

- In contrast, bear markets had a much shorter average duration of 11.5 months but came with a steeper average loss of 30.9%.

This data reaffirms the age-old adage: while market downturns are inevitable, they are often outpaced by extended periods of growth. Let's unpack these patterns further.'

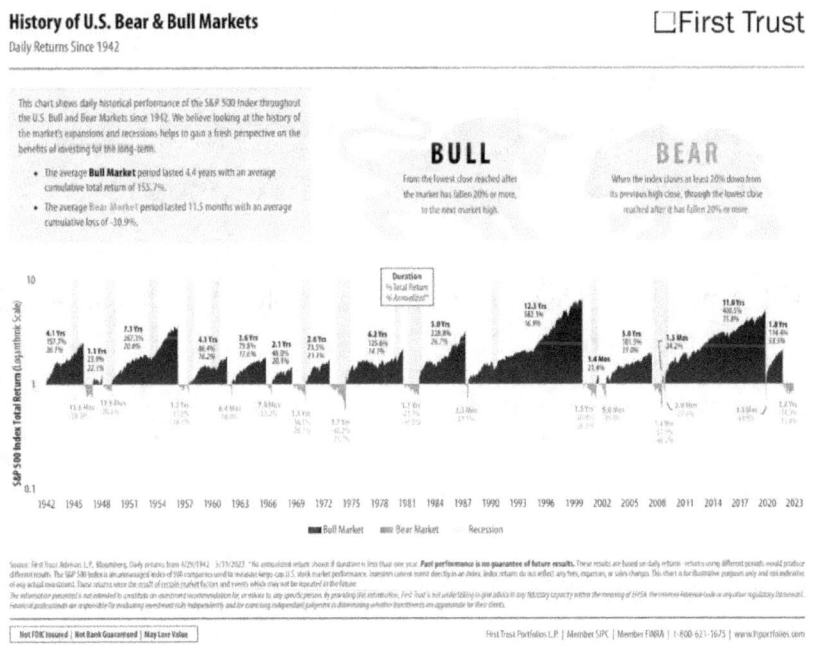

ContentFileLoader.aspx (ftportfolios.com)

Seems straightforward, doesn't it? So, why aren't folks cashing in left, right and centre? Patience. Or rather, the lack of it. As the oracle of Omaha, Warren Buffet, so aptly put it, 'The stock market is a device for transferring money from the impatient to the patient.'

Check out this curious fact: Although the average time people hold onto stocks is less than a year (refer to the graph below), a staggering 80% of investors label themselves as 'long-term'. Something doesn't add up, right? Best of luck deciphering the moves of this 80%! Invest wisely!

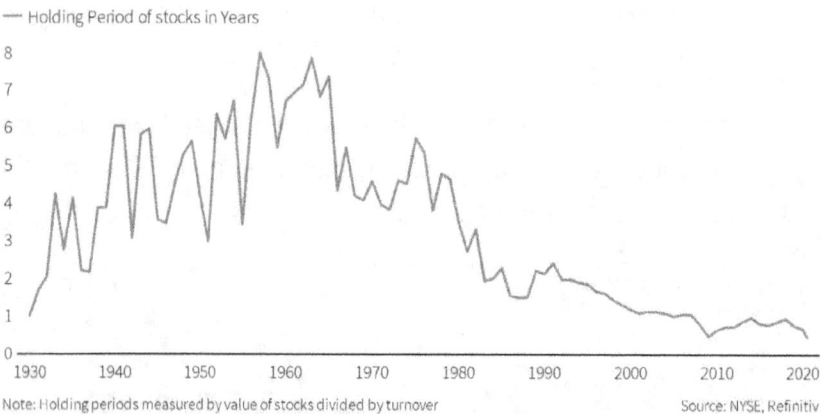

Buy, sell, repeat! No room for 'hold' in whipsawing markets | Reuters

Now that I have explained how the financial and economic environments influence stock prices, let's delve into other essential aspects of investing.

KEY TAKEAWAYS

- 'If it's on the news, it's in the price.' (The exact origin of this phrase is debated, but it's a commonly accepted notion in financial circles.)

- Understand the economic stage to gauge a stock's intrinsic value. This will help to know if a stock can be overvalued.

- Warren Buffet wisely noted that the stock market rewards the patient and penalizes the impatient.

CHAPTER 3
ACTIVE INVESTING
VS.
PASSIVE INVESTING

How do you define success in investing? Is it outperforming the market, achieving consistent and stable returns or building long-term wealth through compounding? Are you comfortable with taking on higher risk, or do you gravitate towards stability and prefer lower risk? These pivotal questions set the stage for understanding the vast realm of investment strategies.

In essence, the methods, strategies and approaches to investing in securities can be distilled into two overarching categories: active investing and passive investing. However, the likes of value investing maestros such as Warren Buffett and Charlie Munger showcase that a blend, a middle ground, also exists, intertwining facets from both realms to garner returns while curbing costs.

Active investing is akin to charting a vessel's course through unpredictable seas. It necessitates a deep dive into market analysis and formulating investment decisions buttressed by rigorous research. Active investors, akin to ships' captains, frequently adjust their sails (buy and sell securities) striving to not just keep pace with but outstrip the market currents. Their eyes are set on capitalizing on fleeting market trends and shifts.

By contrast, passive investing is more of a long-haul voyage. It's about setting a course and letting the natural currents guide you. This often involves anchoring one's investments in broad market indexes like the Dow Jones or the S&P 500. The quintessence of passive investing lies in index funds, which aim to emulate and mirror the performance of these broad market indicators.

Each approach has its pros and cons, especially when considering aspects like fees, tax efficiency, and management. Let's delve deeper.

Benefits of Active Investing

- **Testing the waters** — Active investing is akin to sailing in ever-changing waters, where you constantly have to calibrate your course. This rigorous process not only sharpens one's market acumen but also tests one's ability to navigate and potentially outpace market benchmarks.

- **Agility on deck** — Active investing equips investors with the dexterity to pivot their strategies in tandem with the market's pulse. In stormy financial weather, one might opt for the safety of government bonds, while in a bull run, equities might be the favourable wind.

- **Safety nets and risk calibration** — Active investing empowers investors to jump ship from turbulent sectors or trim their sails when risks escalate. Furthermore, it allows room for hedging — setting up counter-positions to mitigate potential blows from turbulent investments.

- **Strategic tax play** — Active investors, with their frequent trades, have the advantage of tax management. By offsetting gains from profitable ventures with losses, they can potentially reduce the ensuing tax burden.

You may have heard that average investors can't outperform the market, so why bother trying? Well, give a monkey enough darts and they'll beat the market. That's what a draft article by Research Affiliates suggests, citing simulated results of 100 monkeys throwing darts at stock pages. Since 1964, these average monkeys surpassed the index by 1.7% annually. That's a significant bunch of bananas! This monkey business began in 1973 when Princeton University professor Burton Malkiel stated in his bestseller A *Random Walk Down Wall Street* that a blindfolded monkey throwing darts could select a portfolio performing as well as one meticulously chosen by experts.

Research Affiliates tested this by randomly selecting 100 portfolios each containing 30 stocks from a pool of 1,000, annually from 1964 to 2010. Astonishingly, on average, 98 of these monkey-chosen portfolios annually outperformed the capitalization-weighted stock universe.

What's the secret then?

No sorcery here—just mail me $10,000 and I'll send you the finest stock-picking monkey money can buy! Jokes aside, the real magic wasn't in the monkeys or darts but in the predominance of smaller and value stocks outperforming during that period. Typically, any random selection of 30 stocks from 1,000 is likely to include many smaller firms. Since these often outpace larger ones, that's how Malkiel's monkeys beat the market.

Moreover, each of these monkey portfolios was equally weighted. For those new to investing, 'equally weighted' means each stock in the portfolio holds the same proportion, contrary to most market indices where companies with higher market capitalizations dominate. This approach not only lowered the average market cap relative to the cap-weighted index but also amplified returns. Additionally, this equal weighting favored value stocks, which historically yield better returns than growth stocks from 1964 to 2011.

But hold off on rushing to the nearest pet store for a dart-throwing monkey. Higher returns often come with higher risks. Portfolios focusing on smaller-cap and value stocks are riskier than more diversified market portfolios. The 'small-cap premium'—the additional expected return from investing in smaller companies—is well documented. These companies, often less recognized, less global, and less capitalized, inherently carry more risk.

Moreover, these smaller entities typically face higher borrowing costs than larger firms, justifying the higher returns expected by investors.

In upcoming chapters, we will explore strategies to mitigate these risks by not overpaying and regularly monitoring the financial health of your investments. It's also worth noting that monkeys, much like zombies or individuals with cognitive impairments, do not panic in volatile markets, which inadvertently makes them less prone to make fear-driven decisions. Remember, volatility does not always equate to risk, especially if you are investing funds that are not needed in the immediate future—as the saying goes, "never test the depth of the water with both feet." Beware, stocks trading under $1 can indeed turn into a wild jungle.

As we move forward, we'll dive deeper into the realms of passive investing, ETFs, mutual funds, and the strategies of investment legends like Warren Buffett and Peter Lynch. Remember, successful investing isn't just about knowing the price but understanding the value. As Philip Fisher famously said, "The stock market is filled with individuals who know the price of everything but the value of nothing."

↗ Letting the Current Guide You

In contrast to the rigorous, hands-on approach of active investing, passive investing is about setting sail and allowing the broader market currents to direct your journey. At its heart, passive investing revolves around acquiring and retaining assets that mirror broad market indices, such as the Dow Jones Industrial Average or the S&P 500. Within this approach, several vehicles enable investors to embark on this journey, notably mutual funds and exchange-traded funds (ETFs).

- **Mutual funds** – Think of a mutual fund as a collective treasure chest. It gathers resources (money) from a myriad of investors and uses these pooled funds to acquire a diverse range of assets, including stocks and bonds. Expert captains, known as fund managers, steward this treasure trove, ensuring it grows over time.

- **Exchange-traded funds (ETFs)** – ETFs operate similarly to mutual funds but with a twist. Like stocks, they trade on exchanges and emulate the performance of a specific market index, sector or asset class. They combine the versatility of stocks with the broad diversification typical of mutual funds.

The Lure of Passive Investing

- **Gentle on the pocket** – Given that passive investing entails a buy-and-hold ethos, it circumvents the need for intricate analysis and frequent trading. The resultant low churn translates to reduced fees.

- **Sparing the sands of time** – Time is a luxury. Passive investing respects this adage, requiring far less time and effort than its active counterpart. With no pressing need to constantly research or trade, investors find more time to devote to other pursuits.

- **Tax-wise and wise tax** – With infrequent trading, passive investing seldom triggers significant annual capital gains taxes, ensuring tax efficiency.

While considering the broader universe of investment vehicles, it's essential to distinguish between actively and passively managed portfolios. Actively managed funds are the bustling decks of the investment world, always abuzz with activity. Fund managers constantly monitor, analyse and make adjustments, leading to a higher expense ratio – the cost, expressed as a percentage, of owning a mutual fund or ETF. In contrast, the calmer waters of passively managed funds involve minimal intervention and inherently come with a lower expense ratio.

↗ Weighing the Scales

Active and passive strategies present distinct advantages. Your choice hinges on a few guiding questions:

1. Do you have the bandwidth to immerse yourself in market analysis and evaluate stocks meticulously?
2. Are you comfortable embracing higher risks?
3. Does your knowledge arsenal equip you to decode the nuances of financial markets?

If your inner compass resonates with an affirmative to these queries, the whirlwind world of active investing beckons. Otherwise, the steadier, more measured realm of passive investing, with its reduced risk and hands-off approach, might be your ideal harbour.

Remember, whether you choose to constantly adjust your sails or let the winds chart your course, the essence lies in understanding your journey and ensuring it aligns with your destination.

↗ Blending Strategies: The Value Investing Paradigm

The investing spectrum, ranging from the intense scrutiny of active investing to the laissez-faire stance of passive investing, is vast and varied. Yet, nestled between these two lies a harmonious blend that champions both research and restraint. This nuanced approach, celebrated by investing maestros like Warren Buffett and Charlie Munger, is known as value investing.

The ethos of value investing revolves around a simple but potent premise: Identify fundamentally strong businesses, invest in them, and then, display the patience of a monk. This means spotting companies with robust business models, unmatched competitive advantages, and leadership teams that inspire trust, and then holding onto these investments with unwavering conviction, letting time and compounding weave their magic.

The Luminous Lure of Value Investing

Eyes on the horizon: Unlike those swayed by the ebb and flow of short-term market movements, value investors are visionaries. They're in it for the long haul, believing in the enduring promise of a business rather than transient market sentiment.

Economical efficiency: The buy-and-hold mantra doesn't just underscore patience; it also echoes prudence. Infrequent trading means fewer transaction fees, ensuring more of your money remains invested.

Tax-friendly tenure: The taxation realm rewards the patient. With value investing, the long-term stance means that investors often benefit from reduced tax rates on long-term capital gains, compared to their short-term counterparts.

Stability in storms: In the tempestuous seas of the stock market, value stocks often act as anchors. Given their inherent quality, they tend to be less volatile, ensuring the investor's portfolio remains relatively steady amidst market storms.

The compounding conquest: Time, when combined with interest, becomes an investor's most potent ally. Value investors, with their prolonged investment horizons, capitalize on compounding, where returns earned are reinvested to generate their own returns.

While the glittering track record of Buffett and Munger stands as a testament to the prowess of value investing, it's imperative to remember that this isn't a one-size-fits-all blueprint. Every investor's journey is shaped by their unique aspirations, risk appetite, and commitment level. As with any voyage, success in investing isn't about mimicking another's path but about charting one that aligns with your compass. Whether you're drawn to the meticulous analysis of active investing, the serene steadiness of passive strategies, or the blended brilliance of value investing, the key lies in understanding and embracing your chosen approach.

↗ A Dance of Dynamics: Melding Active and Passive Strategies

A quintessential dialogue in the investing arena often revolves around the intrinsic debate between the energy of active investing and the equanimity of passive strategies. Yet, the fascinating blend of both approaches underscores a pivotal realization – the hunt for promising stocks is intrinsically active, but once captured, they're often held with passive tenacity.

In this context, the opinions of renowned market players serve as illuminating torches. Peter Lynch, celebrated for his formidable returns managing Fidelity's Magellan Fund, voiced concerns over the escalating dominance of passive investing in 2021. On the flip side, the Oracle of Omaha, Warren Buffett, placed a significant wager in 2007, betting that the S&P 500 index fund would surpass the performance of actively managed hedge funds over a decade, considering all costs. As history has it, by the close of 2017, he emerged victorious.

However, it's worth noting that while Lynch's track record is awe-inspiring, he remains an anomaly. Overstepping market averages is a Herculean challenge, albeit not an insurmountable one. Individual investors have the agility to delve into niches like small-cap stocks or embrace volatile sectors that might be off-limits to colossal funds. But treading such paths necessitates not just knowledge, but also an unwavering temperament and copious amounts of patience.

The burgeoning influx of novice investors often stokes the flames of market volatility, with many being fixated on prices rather than discerning the intrinsic value of assets. To borrow from the wisdom of Philip Fisher, it's as though the market teems with those versed in the price tags of everything, but unaware of their true worth.

Citing a report from the Wall Street Journal, Buffett's pick, the Vanguard 500 Index Fund Admiral Shares, yielded a 7.1% compounded annual return. In stark contrast, Ted Seides' assortment of hedge funds clocked an average of a mere 2.2%. This juxtaposition between the performance of Lynch and Buffett, two stalwarts who hold mutual respect, exemplifies the diversity in investment philosophies. It underscores that the terrain of investing isn't monolithic; there isn't a single ordained path to triumph.

Of increasing significance today is the recognition that with many ETFs being weighted towards blue-chip enterprises and the surge in index fund investors, there's an intriguing proposition on the horizon. Marrying the dynamism of active stock selection with the patience of passive holding can potentially offer a balanced, potent strategy. This approach, which endorses the idea of investing in robust enterprises while curbing transactional costs, mirrors the ethos shared by Terry Smith: 'Investing can be straightforward – pinpoint commendable firms, ensure you aren't overpaying, and then, simply let time do its work.'

KEY TAKEAWAYS

The realm of investing is rife with choices and strategies:

- **Active Investing** — A spirited dance with the markets, often led by research and swayed by trends. This involves a proactive approach where investors frequently buy and sell securities based on in-depth research, market analysis, and short-term trends. The aim often is to outperform the broader market.

- **Passive Investing** — A calm waltz in which you serenely move in sync with broader market rhythms. This method entails a more hands-off strategy, focusing on long-term growth through investment in broad market indices. It's often characterized by minimal trading, which leads to lower transaction costs and potential tax efficiencies.

- **Value Investing, A Fusion of Active and Passive** — A strategic tango, merging the zest of active selection with the endurance of passive holding. At its core, value investing could be seen as the perfect blend of active and passive strategies.

- **Active Component:** Investors actively seek out and identify undervalued or overlooked stocks. This requires significant research, understanding of the business, and foresight about its future prospects.

- **Passive Component:** Once these 'gems' are discovered, investors often adopt a buy-and-hold strategy, patiently waiting for the market to recognize the true value of these stocks, which sometimes takes years.

- **Intrinsic Value and Market Dynamics:** Value investors bank on the belief that the market sometimes misprices stocks. They posit that, over time, the market will correct this discrepancy, allowing the stock to reach its intrinsic value. This waiting game is where the passive element shines.

- **A Personalized Approach:** There's no one-size-fits-all in investing. The best strategy often depends on an individual's financial goals, risk tolerance, market expertise and time commitment. While the fusion approach of value investing has its merits, it may not align with everyone's perspective or investment philosophy.

- The perfect routine, however, is a deeply personal choice, moulded by individual goals, appetites for risk and dedication to the art of investing.

- Imagine that you're a farmer. You've planted fruit trees, nurtured them, and anticipate a bountiful harvest but nature has its way of testing your patience. Perhaps it doesn't rain enough, or maybe the birds are particularly fond of your fruits this year, leading to a poor yield. Such unexpected, unforeseen events in the financial world are often referred to as 'black swan' events – occurrences that deviate beyond what is normally expected and are difficult to predict.

- Now, let's revert to your tree. If you know in your heart that the tree is fundamentally healthy, would you chop it down and start anew because of one disappointing season? Probably not. Just as a farmer trusts the vitality of a robust tree, you, as an investor, must trust the inherent strength of a good business.

- If the foundation is solid, there's every reason to believe in its long-term potential. Just as you ensure the health of a tree or a plant, ensuring the health of a business is crucial. In the coming chapters, we'll dive deeper into how you can assess the health of a business, ensuring you don't prematurely 'chop down' a promising investment. So, stick around and, more importantly, stay invested.

CHAPTER 4

THE CONSERVATIVE INVESTOR AND COMMON STOCK - GENERAL RULES FOR INVESTING

"If you don't have leverage, you don't get in trouble. That's the only way a smart person can go broke, basically. And I've always said, "If you're smart, you don't need it; and if you're dumb, you shouldn't be using it."

– Warren Buffett

Now that you have a better grasp of the previous chapters of how economic markets operate and a deeper understanding of investment strategies, you might have distilled a key lesson: invest for the long term. It sounds simple, right? Just sit back and wait and eventually, the market currents will transport you to Treasure Island, laden with untold riches.

However, as you sit in your metaphorical boat, bobbing on the waves of the financial sea, understand that patience isn't the only virtue required. The seas of investing can be unpredictable, and to ensure you don't end up wrecked at the bottom of the ocean, some navigational rules are vital.

Importantly, stay debt-free. Playing with borrowed money or money you might need urgently is a recipe for disaster. Debts and unexpected expenses can compromise your long-term perspective. Ideally, the only debt on your books should be for your primary residence.

Also, think things through and ask yourself these pivotal questions. How long can you keep your money invested? Are you after quick profits or generational wealth? Do market downturns send you into panic mode, or do you view them as discount shopping days? As a novice investor, it's essential to frame your approach around these pivotal questions.

Realise that investing is more than just numbers; it's an art form that demands an in-depth understanding of businesses to nurture value and build wealth. Remember Warren Buffett's wise saying, 'Price is what you pay. Value is what you get.' The true essence of a stock isn't in its momentary price but in the underlying business's growth and prosperity.

While there isn't a one-size-fits-all investing rulebook, some time-tested guidelines can help rookies minimize the number of icebergs they hit. But first, a quick glossary to get you familiar with the lingo:

Glossary

- **Bulls:** Optimistic investors who believe in and often drive the market's upward trajectory.
- **Bears:** Pessimistic investors forecasting a market drop, thereby leading to potential downtrends.
- **Rally:** A sustained uptick in stock prices after a dip or consolidation.
- **Volatility:** A measure of price variation for a stock or market, indicative of risk and uncertainty.
- **Correction:** A transient drop in stock prices post a high point, is often seen as a market's healthy adjustment.
- **Market Capitalization:** The cumulative value of a company's floating shares, ascertained by multiplying the stock price by its available shares.
- **Blue-chip Stocks:** Stocks from established, financially sound corporations with a proven performance track record.
- **Short Selling:** Offloading borrowed stocks expecting a price dip, intending to purchase them back cheaper to turn a profit.
- **Dividend:** A slice of a company's profits shared with its shareholders, a token of gratitude for their trust.
- **Liquidity:** The ease with which assets can be bought or sold without markedly altering their price.

By no means is this an exhaustive blueprint for investing, but adhering to some of the following fundamental principles will significantly improve your odds in the long game of investing.

I am not going to lay down an exhaustive list of rules for investing, but certain basic rules of investing must be followed to stay in the game for the long run.

1. **Think for the long term.**

    The stock market can be capricious in the short term, as it's often influenced by sentiment and speculation. Yet, as Warren Buffett paraphrased Ben Graham in 1987: 'In the short run, a market is a voting machine, but in the long run, it is a weighing machine.' The fundamental idea expressed here is that stock prices will, over time, align with the company's actual value or fundamentals. In the short term, speculation and sentiment might cause deviations, but in the grander scheme, the true value will manifest.

    This sentiment is echoed in Warren Buffett's assertion that the stock market is a 'transaction of money from the impatient to the patient.'

    The graph below explains why staying in the market long-term is important. You can see that the more time you are in, the greater the possibility of making positive returns as you don't get affected by intermittent market fluctuations.

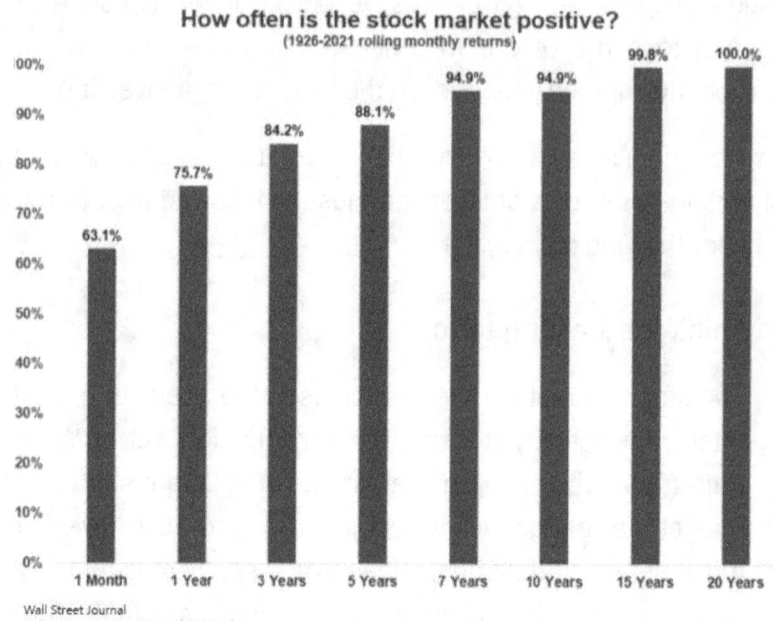

Source: investing.com

S&P 500: 1926-2015

Time Frame	Positive	Negative
Daily	54%	46%
Quarterly	68%	32%
One Year	74%	26%
5 Years	86%	14%
10 Years	94%	6%
20 Years	100%	0%

Source: Returns 2.0

Over one year, most stock price fluctuations are driven by changes in valuation. However, in the long run, stock prices are driven by the evolution of the intrinsic value of a company.

> *"In the short term the stock market behaves like a voting machine, but in the long term it acts as a weighing machine."* – Benjamin Graham

This means that in the short term, the valuation you pay for a company is very important while in the long term, the rate at which a company can grow its earnings per share is the crucial factor.

'If you bought the S&P 500 at a P/E of 5.3x in 1917, and sold it in 1999 at a P/E of 34x, your annual return would have been 11.6%. Only 2.3% p.a. came from the massive increase in P/E. The rest of your return came from the companies' earnings and reinvestments.' – Terry Smith

You've already learned that you want to buy stocks at cheap valuation levels. However, just because something is cheap doesn't make it a good value. In the stock market, it is never a good idea to buy a stock just because it looks cheap.

Let's get back to 2010 and take 2 examples. In 2010, S&P Global was trading at a P/E of 19.3 while General Electric was trading at a P/E of 15.3. Purely based on this information, you would say that General Electric is the more interesting investment because the company is valued more attractively.

Well... things turned out quite differently. Since 2010 S&P Global's stock price increased by more than 2100% while General Electric's stock only increased by 100%. What is the reason for this?

When looking at the valuation of a company, you should always take other factors into account. Think about the return on invested capital (ROIC) for example.

It can be justified to pay a higher multiple for a stock when the company is fundamentally healthier. In our example, we notice that S&P Global is the better company by far. From 2010 until today, S&P Global reported an average ROIC of 27.4% compared to only 2.2% for General Electric.

2. **The first $100k is the most difficult.**

The journey to your first $100k is arguably the most challenging in the world of investing. This initial phase requires immense discipline, a steadfast mindset, and navigation through the initial learning curves. Charlie Munger once highlighted this hurdle, emphasizing the importance of even underspending one's income to reach this milestone.

Accumulating the first $100k is the hardest part of creating wealth. Then, the next big hurdle is the first million but an individual needs to find a way to do that even if it means underspending his income.

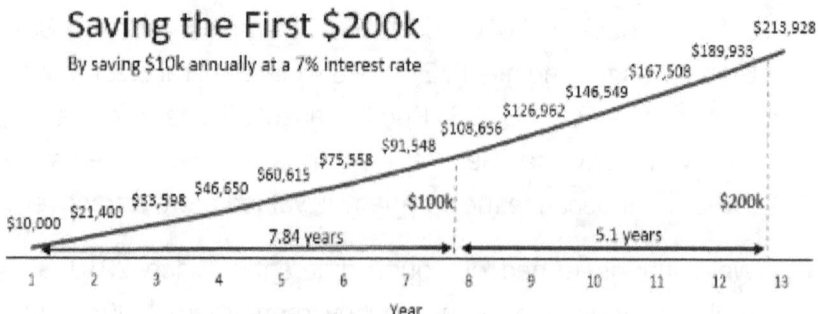

Source: https://bluebellpwm.com/

The graph above will help you to understand the point. You can see that investing $10K annually at 7% (on a conservative basis considering the average annual return on the S&P 500 index for the last five years from 2018-2022 is 9.27%) would take you 7.84 years to get to your first $100K, while the second $100K would take you only 5.1 years.

3. Learn from past mistakes.

It is important to learn from your past mistakes but be wise enough to learn from others' mistakes. Things often go wrong in life, but that does not mean the end of the world. You need to constantly keep learning and avoid repeating the same errors. When it comes to investing, you can often go wrong when assessing the stock's intrinsic value and end up overpaying for it. Sometimes, the company whose stock you hold may not grow as you projected it would. However, that's all good and it's part of the investing game. Just accept and learn from it by pinpointing what went wrong in your assessment.

4. Market corrections can be windows of opportunity.

Market cycles, as we explored in the second chapter, mirror economic cycles. Every market correction brings with it golden chances to procure quality stocks at more palatable prices. As Benjamin Graham insightfully noted in The Intelligent Investor, 'The intelligent investor is a realist who sells to optimists and buys from pessimists.' The market is driven by the sentiments of greed and fear. When greed overpowers, the stocks tend to become exorbitantly expensive, and the same stocks trade at very cheap prices when the sentiment of fear looms large. The markets are bound to correct, and an intelligent investor sees opportunities in the adversity of pessimism. Market corrections are inevitable, but to the astute investor, they also offer lucrative opportunities.

Summary of Market Corrections

- Market cycles are often linked with economic cycles.
- Market corrections provide opportunities to purchase high-quality stocks at a discounted rate.
- An intelligent investor buys during pessimistic periods and sells during optimistic periods.

5. Be an investor, not a speculator.

It is a common phenomenon that many newcomers to the investment world find themselves speculating, swayed by the constant deluge of news and tips. Speculation can yield results on a few lucky occasions but does not help much over the long run. Investing requires patience and knowledge that helps to analyse the situation better and make good investment decisions. Joel Greenblatt explained the simple investment strategy that helped him generate 33% annually between 1988 and 2004 in his book The Little Book That Beats the Market. His investment strategy was based on the simple principle, 'Buy good companies that are cheap.' He focused on buying companies with a combination of the earnings yield (cheap or expensive) with the highest return on capital (how good the company is). You will learn more about earnings yield in the subsequent chapter, where we dive deeper into financial metrics to assess the financial strength of the companies.

6. Value and growth form the investment equilibrium.

Investment equilibrium is achieved when an investor skilfully balances growth prospects with inherent value. It is important to consider both growth and value aspects when evaluating investment opportunities. 'Growth without value becomes speculation, but value without growth becomes a value trap.'

Focusing solely on growth potential without considering the underlying value can lead to speculative investments with inflated prices. On the other hand, solely focusing on value without considering growth prospects may result in investing in companies or assets that are undervalued for a reason and may not experience significant appreciation over time. Striking a balance between growth and value is key to making sound investment decisions.

'When things go wrong with value traps, investors have a level of protection from tangible assets, cash, and dividends.

But

When things go wrong with growth traps, investors are wholly dependent on the kindness of strangers...'

7. **Time in the market trumps timing the market.**

François Rochon, one of the best quality investors, rightly pointed this out. 'Timing the market' generally refers to buying stocks when they have bottomed out and selling them when they have reached their peak. 'Market bottoming out' refers to the forthcoming upside reversal resulting in the rise of stock prices after a significant market correction. Market peaking refers to the forthcoming downside reversal where the prices start falling after significant upside movement. No one, absolutely no one, can exactly predict and catch the market bottom and peak, and hence, there seems to be no point in wasting time in trying to do so. One should rather invest efforts in finding companies with high returns and high margins and build an investment strategy focused on holding onto quality stocks. Rochon's portfolio stocks returned a staggering 2817% from 1996 to 2021, making an annualized return of 13.9%. Hence, we can safely take his advice that time in the market is always better than timing the market.

DON'T TRY TO TIME THE MARKET

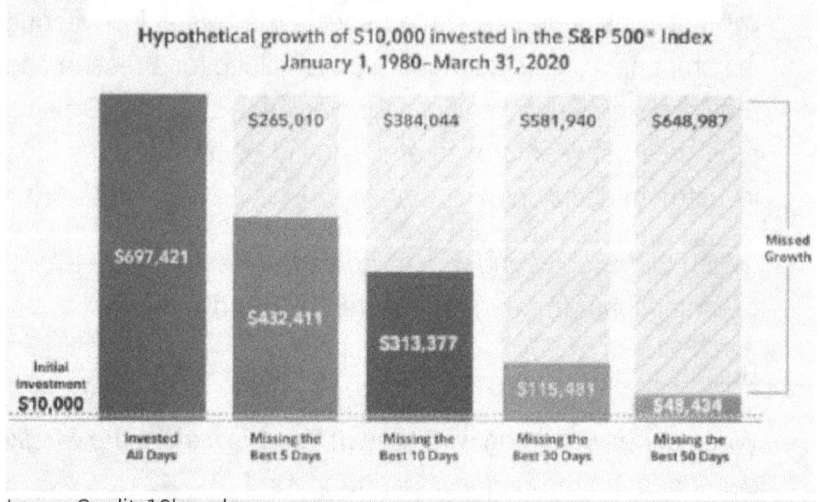

Image Credit: 10kreader

8. Know the business you own.

When you invest, it means that you take ownership of a piece of the business that the stock represents. The more pieces of the business you own, the more benefits you get. Hence, you must understand the business you intend to invest in and focus on investing in the area of your competence.

For example, consider the rise and fall of Blockbuster, once the dominant force in video rentals. Many investors saw it as a stable business with a pervasive physical presence. However, they failed to see the technological disruption on the horizon in the form of digital streaming and online rentals. Netflix, an upstart at that time, understood the shifting dynamics and adapted its business model to capitalize on it. Investors who failed to understand these nuances and the changing landscape of entertainment consumption faced significant losses as Blockbuster filed for bankruptcy, while Netflix became a dominant player in the industry. This underscores the importance of truly understanding the business you're investing in, along with the larger industry trends.

Joel Greenblatt wisely said, 'Choosing individual stocks without any idea of what you're looking for is like running through a dynamite factory with a burning match. You may live, but you're still an idiot.'

Here are some fundamental tenets you should be considering:

- **Is the business model understandable?** Venture into businesses that you can comfortably fathom. If you're unclear about their operational blueprint, revenue generation, or industry dynamics, you're starting on shaky ground.

- **Are the company's long-term prospects favourable?** Peek into the future. Does the company have resilient competitive advantages, growth trajectories, and the agility to adapt to consumer needs?

- **Has the company shown operational consistency?** History often hints at the future. If a company has demonstrated steadiness across economic terrains, it's a positive sign.

- **Does the business enjoy a high entry threshold?** Barriers to entry safeguard a business's position. Elements like proprietary technology, formidable brand reputation, or economies of scale can buffer against potential competitors.

- **How competent and transparent is the management?** The company's helmsmen matter. Their track record, strategic prowess, and integrity steer the company's direction. We'll delve deeper into this in Chapter 6.

- **Is the return on equity satisfactory?** ROE illustrates how efficiently a company converts shareholder capital into profits. A comparative analysis with industry standards can be enlightening. More on this in Chapter 5.

- **Are the company's profit margins appealing?** Profit margins act as a thermometer for a company's operational efficiency and pricing authority. A comparative look with industry benchmarks can yield useful insights.

9. **Always buy stocks at a discount.**

    When you go to the mall, you like to buy your favourite products on sale. Can you buy the toothpaste you always use at a 30% discount? Or is there a special action on your favourite beer? That's lovely. Let's buy some extra toothpaste and beer. The same goes for stocks. You want to buy a stock at its cheapest possible price and valuation. The beautiful thing about the stock market is that Mr. Market often acts as a manic-depressive. You can use this volatility to your advantage.

    For almost all stocks, the difference between the lowest and highest stock price in a certain year is larger than 50%. You don't believe me? Let's take S&P Global as an example. The lowest stock price of the past 52 weeks was equal to $279 while the highest stock price over the same period was equal to $450. A difference of 61%.

This checklist, while not exhaustive, furnishes an overarching lens to assess prospective investments. Every investment journey, however, demands meticulous research tailored to the company and industry in question. With time, you can cultivate and refine your own set of business tenets to streamline your investment journey.

Glossary

- Return on Equity (ROE): A measure of a company's profitability that compares its net income to its shareholders' equity. It indicates how well the company is using shareholders' funds to generate earnings. A higher ROE indicates that the company generates more profits for its shareholders.

- Portfolio Diversification: The practice of spreading investments among different securities or sectors to reduce risk.

⤴ Factor in all costs associated with your investments.

Your net investment outcomes are inevitably shaped by the cumulative costs and taxes that chip away at your returns. The mantra? Minimize these drags. Heeding Benjamin Graham's wisdom: 'If fees nibble away more than 1% of your assets annually, it's time to reconsider your advisor.' As discussed previously, the cost structures of active and passive investment strategies differ. One way to optimize outflows is by holding onto investments for prolonged periods. This approach not only tempers capital gain taxes but also curbs frequent transactional costs.

↗ Create a healthy portfolio diversification: The paradox of choice.

We have all heard the proverb, 'Don't put all your eggs into one basket.; The same applies to investing, as you cannot risk putting all your hard-earned money in one particular stock, sector, or asset class. We will be dealing with the concept of portfolio diversification in detail later in Chapter 9. First, however, to introduce you to the concept, portfolio diversification refers to spreading your investments across different stocks and sectors or even different asset classes. It is also important to understand the degree of correlation between the different securities in the portfolio to arrive at the optimal. Thus, you can understand portfolio diversification as a method of mitigating risk.

Easy right? Hold your horses! Warren Buffett, the investing maestro, once said, 'Diversification is protection against ignorance.' Let's not misinterpret this as a slight. Buffett's wisdom holds a kernel of audacity that shakes up the traditional diversification playbook. Sure, diversifying is wise—it's like having a safety net as you walk the tightrope of the stock market. But here's the twist: if you've done your homework, you don't need to spread your investments across the board.

So, what's the middle ground? Aim for focused diversification. Think of it as a well-curated art collection rather than a crowded gallery where masterpieces lose their allure. Pick your assets shrewdly, understand their potential, and keep an eye on them—quality trumps quantity every time. Aim for a portfolio that's diverse enough to be resilient, yet focused enough to capitalize on your knowledge—because in the end, an informed conviction can be the investor's truest ally.

↗ Manage the risk.

Investing in no way means avoiding risk altogether. Rather, it means managing the risk well so that your portfolio does not fall significantly in adverse market conditions. In addition, different securities and different asset classes have varying degrees of risk. For example, treasuries, gold, and cash are less risky than stocks. Hence, investing means mitigating the overall portfolio risk with a combination of different securities, thereby creating an optimal portfolio.

Risk management is important because, during adverse market conditions, people tend to shift their money from equities to safer assets like gold. Thus, too much concentration on one particular security or asset class can backfire tremendously when that particular sector or industry is in jeopardy. Hence, creating an optimal portfolio by mitigating the risk enables one to perform better over the long run and be the least affected in adverse market conditions. We will understand more about risk management in Chapter 9 when we deal with portfolio diversification and managing risk in investing.

KEY TAKEAWAYS

- Think for the long term and focus on the company's long-term prospects and intrinsic value.

- Market corrections offer opportunities; hence, look to buy quality stocks at discounted prices.

- Balance between growth and value when evaluating investments.

- Time in the market is better than timing the market to generate compounding returns.

- Know your business and understand the company's model, prospects and management.

- Create a diversified portfolio to spread investments to mitigate risk.

- Diversification is an investment strategy that prescribes investing in a series of asset classes, companies and sectors.

- An investor who diversifies their holdings can minimize their losses and risk.

- Diversification has some downsides such as missing out on potential gains in search of less risk.

- Diversification may also lead to higher transaction fees and an overreliance on a financial advisor for more complex portfolios.

CHAPTER 5
FINANCIAL METRICS TO GAUGE COMPANY'S FINANCIAL STRENGTH

"The key to making money in stocks is not to get scared out of them."

– Peter Lynch

Financial Metrics to Gauge Company's Financial Strength

Welcome to the Dunning-Kruger theme park, where the first ride is the Overconfidence Rollercoaster—strapping you in with a 'This is easy!' and then doing a loop-de-loop into 'This is actually quite difficult.' Don't worry, it's normal to feel like you've forgotten how to read for a minute. If you hit the 'I'll never understand' dip, just remember that's part of the thrill.

As you chug up to the 'Getting the hang of it' hill, give yourself a pat on the back. You're now a savvy explorer in the jungle of knowledge, swinging past the 'Trust me, this isn't easy' vines. If the trail gets too wild, backtrack is your friend—those previous chapters are like breadcrumbs to guide you home. Keep your humour hat on tight, and let's keep trekking!

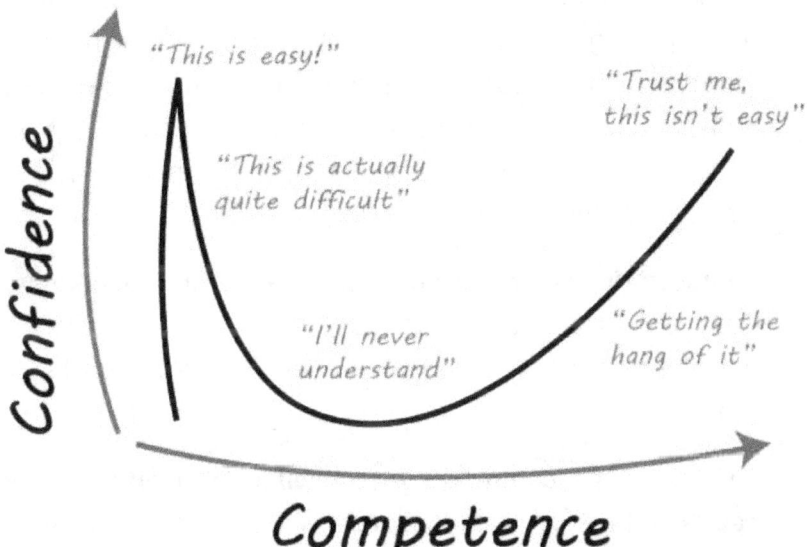

Source: Dunning-Kruger Effect: Recognising your knowledge gap (asprayfranchise.co.uk)

Now that we've covered the fundamentals of investing, it's essential to evaluate a company's financial strength and growth potential before considering an investment. The financial strength of a company is assessed through various financial ratios, which provide insights into the company's liquidity, debt levels, market valuation, future growth prospects and competitive position in the market. These ratios are often referred to as 'accounting ratios' and are derived from the company's financial statements, including the balance sheet, income statement and cash flow statement.

Financial professionals calculate these ratios for several reasons.

- **To measure profit margins and identify profitability trends:** Ratios like profit margin percentages help in understanding how efficiently a company converts its sales into profits over time. This can reveal trends in profitability.

- **To measure working capital funding requirements:** Remember that working capital is the efficiency with which a company generates profits from its assets. A higher ROA indicates that the company uses its assets more effectively. Working capital ratios assess the amount of capital required to fund the day-to-day operations of the company, providing insights into its short-term liquidity.

- **To ascertain the amount of debt used to fund operations:** Debt ratios reveal the extent to which a company relies on borrowed funds to finance its activities, helping assess its risk profile.

- **To assess the company's effectiveness in using working capital:** Efficiency ratios, such as inventory turnover, measure how effectively a company utilizes its working capital to generate sales.

- **To measure the company's ability to settle short-term and long-term debt and liabilities:** Solvency ratios assess the company's ability to meet its short-term and long-term debt obligations.

To better understand these financial ratios, let's first clarify some key terms that are essential components of financial statements.

Glossary

- **Assets:** Assets represent valuable possessions or resources owned by the company. Just as in your personal life, where assets might include your car, laptop or clothes, in business, assets are categorized into:
- **Current assets:** These are assets that can be quickly converted into cash, usually within a year. Examples include cash, cash equivalents (like short-term bonds), marketable securities, accounts receivable and inventory.
- **Non-current assets:** These are assets that cannot be easily converted to cash or are not expected to be converted within a year. Examples include property, plant and equipment (PPE), long-term investments, and intangible assets like patents and goodwill.
- **Liabilities:** Liabilities represent the debts or financial obligations owed by the company. Just as in your personal life, liabilities can be categorized into:
- **Current liabilities:** These are debts or obligations due within a short period, typically a year. Examples include accounts payable, short-term loans, salaries payable and other obligations expected to be settled within a year.
- **Non-current liabilities:** These are debts or obligations not due within the next year. Examples include bonds payable, long-term loans, deferred tax liabilities and other long-term financial obligations.
- **Equity:** Equity represents the net value of assets after deducting liabilities. It's similar to an individual's or a

company's net worth. If you subtract the total debts (liabilities) from the total assets, you get the equity. For instance, if a house is worth $300,000, and there's a mortgage (debt) of $200,000 on it, the equity in the house is $100,000.

Understanding these terms and the financial ratios derived from them will be crucial as we explore how to assess a company's financial strength and make informed investment decisions.

↗ Equity vs. Capitalization

When a company enters the stock market, its equivalent term is 'capitalization'. Capitalization is the total value of a company derived from its share price multiplied by the total number of outstanding shares.

Now, you might wonder why these terms matter. In an ideal world, equity and capitalization should align, but in reality, they often don't. People may pay more or less than a company's equity value, influenced by expectations of future growth.

↗ Understanding the Price-to-Book (P/B) Ratio

To make sense of this, we introduce the Price-to-Book (P/B) ratio, a key metric for investors. The P/B ratio compares the current market price of a company's stock (capitalization) to its book value (equity). It's calculated as follows:

$$P/B = \frac{\text{Book Value per Share}}{\text{Market Price per Share}} = \frac{\textbf{Shareholder's Equity}}{\textbf{Capitalization}}$$

Here's what this means:

Market price per share: This is the current trading price of a company's stock in the market. It represents what investors are willing to pay.

Book value per share: This is the value of the company's equity divided by the number of outstanding shares. It represents the net asset value of the company per share, essentially what each share would be worth if the company were liquidated.

Now, let's relate this to our earlier discussion.

If the P/B ratio is greater than 1, it suggests that investors are willing to pay more for the company's equity (book value) than what's stated on the balance sheet. This might be due to high growth expectations.

If the P/B ratio is less than 1, it implies that investors are paying less for the company's equity than its book value. This could indicate that the market has undervalued the company.

Understanding Earnings and Net Income

A company's growth is closely tied to its earnings. Just as your gross salary isn't the same as your net income after taxes, a company's earnings don't tell the whole story. We focus on net income, which is akin to your take-home pay.

Let's simplify this with everyday examples. Think of your gross salary as a company's earnings before expenses and taxes. Your net income is what you have left after all deductions. Similarly, a company's net income is what it retains after expenses and taxes.

↗ Using Net Income for Return Ratios

Investors often use net income to calculate return ratios, such as Return on Equity (ROE) and Return on Assets (ROA). A higher return is generally seen as better. However, there's a catch.

In the ideal world where capitalization equals equity, a higher ROE is favourable. However, if you're paying more than a company's equity value, you need to consider that.

↗ Understanding Return Ratios

Return ratios, like ROE and ROA, are critical in assessing a company's efficiency at generating profit relative to its equity and assets, respectively. Generally, a higher return ratio is viewed positively as it indicates a more efficient use of resources.

↗ The role of net income

Net income is a key figure for calculating return ratios. For ROE, the formula is:

$$ROE = \frac{\text{Net Income}}{\text{Shareholder's Equity}}$$

This formula helps investors understand how well the company is generating income relative to the equity invested by shareholders.

↗ The Impact of Price-to-Book (P/B) Ratio

The P/B ratio compares a company's market capitalization to its book value. A P/B ratio above 1 can indicate that the market values the company more than its equity value, whereas a P/B ratio below 1 suggests the opposite.

An example: Company A vs. Company B

Let's break down the example with Company A and Company B to understand how the P/B ratio affects the perceived ROE.

Company A:

P/B Ratio: 2 (You're paying twice x2 (100%) the equity value)

ROE: 30%

Adjusting the ROE for the P/B ratio gives us an adjusted ROE, calculated as follows:

$$\text{Adjusted ROE} = \frac{\text{ROE}}{\text{P/B Ratio}} = \frac{30\%}{2} = 15\%$$

This adjustment shows that considering the price you're paying relative to the equity value (P/B ratio), the effective return (adjusted ROE) is 15%.

Company B:

P/B Ratio: 0.8 (You're paying 80% of the equity value. 20% discount)

ROE: 30%

Again, adjusting the ROE for the P/B ratio:

$$\text{Adjusted ROE} = \frac{\text{ROE}}{\text{P/B Ratio}} = \frac{30\%}{2} = 37.5\%$$

Here, because the P/B ratio is below 1, indicating that you're paying less than the company's equity value, the effective return on your investment increases to 37.5%.

This example illustrates an important consideration when evaluating investments using ROE. The P/B ratio can significantly influence the attractiveness of an ROE figure. A higher ROE might not always be favourable once adjusted for the company's valuation relative to its book value, as seen with Company A.

Conversely, Company B, with a P/B ratio below 1 presents a more attractive adjusted ROE, suggesting that investors are getting more value for their investment relative to the company's equity.

Alright, we've discussed net income, but what about earnings? What role do they play?

The current P/E ratio of a company is calculated by dividing the current market price of a company's stock by its earnings per share (EPS). For instance, if a company's stock is trading at $100 and the EPS for the past 12 months is $5, then the P/E ratio is 20 ($100 / $5 = 20). This means investors are willing to pay $20 for every $1 of earnings, which gives you an idea of how much value the market is placing on the company's future growth and profitability.

To gauge whether a stock is overvalued or undervalued, investors often compare the current P/E ratio with the average P/E ratio of the industry or the overall market. If the company's P/E is higher than the industry or market average, it suggests that investors are expecting higher earnings growth in the future compared to peers. Conversely, a lower P/E might indicate that the stock is undervalued relative to the earnings it generates.

However, the P/E ratio should not be viewed in isolation. It's essential to consider other factors such as the company's growth prospects, the industry it operates in and the economic environment. For example, a high P/E ratio might be justified for a tech startup with rapidly growing earnings, while a mature utility company might typically have a lower P/E ratio due to steady but slower growth.

Investors also use the P/E ratio to determine the relative attractiveness of a stock. If a company has a history of steady earnings growth and maintains a P/E ratio below the industry average, it could be seen as a good investment opportunity, assuming that all other factors are favourable.

In essence, the P/E ratio serves as a barometer of market sentiment, providing a quick snapshot of what investors are willing to pay for a stock based on its past or expected future earnings. By comparing a stock's P/E ratio with its historical average, the industry average, or the market as a whole, investors can start to determine whether a stock is priced fairly, or if it's potentially overvalued or undervalued. This comparison, along with a thorough analysis of the company's fundamentals and growth prospects, can help investors make more informed decisions.

Peter Lynch, in his book One Up on Wall Street, simplifies this concept further. He suggests that a company's P/E ratio should ideally match its earnings growth rate. If a company's earnings are expected to increase by 15% in the next year, a P/E ratio of 15 would indicate the stock is fairly priced. So, if you're eyeing a stock like Coca-Cola and its P/E ratio is 15, you'd hope to see the company's earnings chug upwards at about 15% a year.

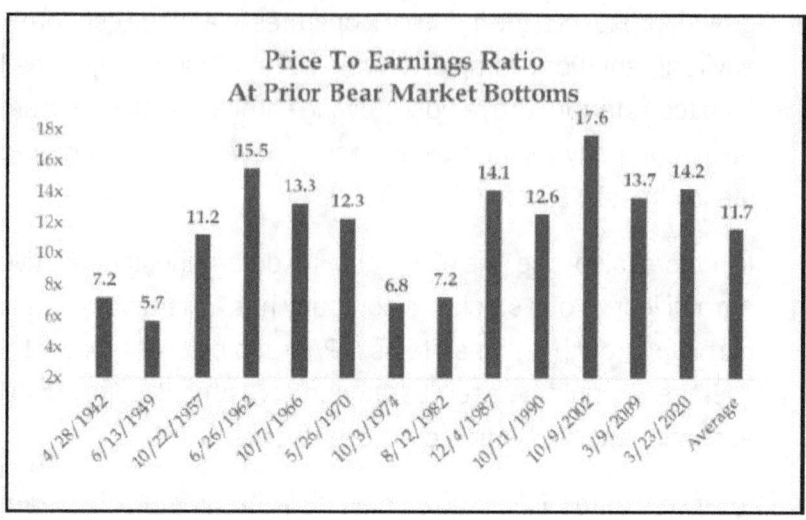

Source: Unknown

Now, let's say you're considering two companies as potential investments. Company A, a '12-percent grower', is increasing its earnings by 12% annually, but it has a P/E ratio of just 6. That's like finding designer shoes at half the price—quite the bargain. On the flip side, Company B is also a '12-percent grower', but its P/E ratio is 24, making it as overpriced as those same designer shoes at a premium boutique.

Lynch points out that a P/E ratio half the growth rate is a green flag for investors, signalling potential value. Conversely, a P/E ratio twice the growth rate could spell trouble, indicating an overvalued stock that might soon fall from grace.

If you're left scratching your head without a growth rate in hand, roll up your sleeves and do some digging. Look up the company's past earnings, do a little math to see how much they've grown from one year to the next, and voilà—you have the growth rate.

Lynch also offers a more nuanced way to look at the P/E ratio by including dividends. Suppose Company X is growing at

12%, pays a dividend yield of 3%, and has a P/E ratio of 10. Add the growth rate and dividend yield, then divide by the P/E ratio: (12% + 3%) / 10 = 1.5. It's like a financial version of your high school GPA—a score below 1 might have your parents frowning, 1.5 is decent, but a score of 2 or more will have you on the honour roll. So, if you spot a company with a 15% growth rate, a 3% dividend yield, and a P/E of 6, you've hit the jackpot with a score of 3—a financial valedictorian.

In summary, the P/E ratio isn't just a number—it's a scale that weighs the price of a stock against the company's earning power, growth potential, and the little extra sweetener of dividends. Just like in any bargain hunting, the goal is to pay less for more. Keep this principle in your investor's toolkit, and you may just find yourself picking stocks with the confidence of a seasoned pro.

Let's demystify the P/E ratio with a practical example. Suppose you're eyeing a property on the market for $100,000 which promises a rental income of $2,000 per year. It doesn't sound very appealing, does it? That's a P/E ratio of 50—akin to buying into the dream that the neighbourhood will boom thanks to government investment, and the property's value will double, if not more, in the future.

Now, consider a different scenario: a house costing $10,000 with a rental return of $1,000 annually. With a P/E ratio of 10, within a decade, you'll have almost recouped your initial outlay. This is the essence of value investing—measuring outlay against return, and thereby managing risk.

Have I passed up on opportunities by avoiding stocks with high P/E ratios? Indeed, sometimes a high P/E can be justified, especially in the nascent stages of a company or within burgeoning markets. However, for behemoths like Apple, with an already expansive market share, astronomical growth isn't just improbable; it would require a Herculean surge in sales—something I'm sceptical of. The prospects of improving services in a remote area might be boundless, but how much more can a prime city centre location appreciate?

The Impact of the Price-to-Earnings (P/E) Ratio: How Not to Overpay

If you buy an apartment in the city center, sure, you can rent it out for a substantial amount, but at what cost? You'll likely pay a premium that includes, if not exceeds, the value of all services. This makes it overvalued. While owning such an apartment can be appealing, it's not necessarily a sound investment. Similarly, purchasing shares in a renowned company doesn't automatically translate to a savvy investment decision.

Certainly, many investors are willing to bet on high P/E ratios for established companies, but it's often those same investors who precipitate a crash, leading to drastic losses. I prefer to sidestep such frenzies. After all, as Warren Buffett cleverly put it, 'Only when the tide goes out do you discover who's been swimming naked.' And when it comes to investing, I'd rather not be caught in the buff.

Additional Terms

1. **Inventories:** This is similar to the stock of goods or resources that you have for future use. In a personal setting, this could be the food stocked up in your pantry or the stationery you have for your home office. In a business setting, inventories could be raw materials, work-in-progress goods, and finished goods ready for sale.

Think of inventories like the contents of your fridge. Ideally, you want a steady flow of groceries in and out. If you see last week's veggies starting to wilt while you continue to pile in fresh ones, you've got a problem—too much stock and not enough consumption. That's a bit like what happens in a company when inventories stack up; it suggests products aren't selling.

When a business accumulates products faster than it's selling, consider it a warning sign—much like milk piling up in your fridge suggests you're not drinking it quickly enough. In the business world, this could mean a future sale or markdown is on the horizon to clear out old stock.

Accounting for inventories can be as varied as kitchen recipes. There's LIFO (Last In, First Out), akin to using the newest milk in your fridge first, leaving the older cartons at the back. Or FIFO (First In, First Out), like using the oldest eggs before they go bad. Whether a company uses LIFO or FIFO can impact how profits are calculated, much like using ingredients purchased at different prices can affect your grocery budget.

Some humorous but less official methods like GIGO (Garbage In, Garbage Out) and FISH (First In, Still Here) are akin to buying low-quality ingredients that ruin a meal or letting things sit unused, like that fancy mixer you bought but never used.

You can measure a company's inventory health by comparing this year's inventory value to last year's, checking if it's grown or shrunk. Imagine visiting a friend whose garage is so crammed with bulk-bought paper towels they have to park their car on the street—it's the same with businesses. For example, if a clothing retailer announces a 10% sales increase but their inventories have swelled by 30%, you might wonder why they didn't have a clearance sale. Without addressing this, they may struggle down the line, much like you'd struggle with an overstocked pantry when next week's grocery deals roll out.

However, not all inventory build-ups spell disaster. For car manufacturers, a build-up isn't as alarming since new models usually retain value—a car that costs $35,000 won't drop to $3,500 overnight. In contrast, fashion is fickle; a $300 purple miniskirt might become nearly worthless once it's out of style.

On the flip side, shrinking inventories in a recovering company can signal a turnaround—like finally seeing the back of your freezer after a long winter. Experienced investors, especially those with a knack for a particular industry, will know how to interpret these signs.

2. **Cash:** Cash is the money readily available to you. It's like the money in your wallet, piggy bank, or checking account. It's the most liquid asset and can be used instantly to purchase goods or services or pay off debts.

Just like you'd feel more comfortable lending a friend money if you knew they had savings, investors feel better about companies with extra cash. It's like a safety net that can also be used to reward everyone involved. Here are some examples of how cash can be a good reward for investors:

Paying dividends: This is like sharing the profits directly with the shareholders. If you own shares, you get a piece of the pie in the form of dividend payments, typically given out quarterly.

Buying back shares: Companies can buy their own shares back from the market. This reduces the number of shares available, which can increase the value of the remaining shares. It's a way to return cash to shareholders indirectly because it can lead to a higher share price.

Paying off debt: Just like paying off a personal loan or credit card frees up more of your budget for other things, when a company pays its debt, it reduces the interest expenses it has to pay. This not only strengthens the company's financial position but can also lead to better credit ratings and lower future borrowing costs.

3. **EBITDA** (Earnings before interest, taxes, depreciation and amortization): This is like your salary before any deductions and a measure of core corporate profitability. It's a measure of earnings from your job before accounting for costs like taxes, social security contributions, health insurance premiums, etc. Similarly, EBITDA in a business setting is a measure of a company's operational profitability before deductions like interest, taxes, and depreciation/amortization.

4. **EBIT** (Earnings before interest and taxes): This is similar to your take-home pay after subtracting all deductions except for taxes and interest expenses. In a business setting, EBIT is the earnings purely from business operations before interest and taxes are deducted.

5. **Prepaid expenses:** These are payments made in advance for goods or services to be received in the future. Consider

it as buying a yearly gym membership. You pay upfront (prepaid expense), and you get the service throughout the year. For a business, this could include things like insurance premiums paid in advance, prepaid rent, etc.

6. **Cash equivalents:** These are investments that can be quickly converted into cash with minimal risk of change in value. Examples in your personal life might be money market funds or short-term government bonds.

7. **Total debt:** This is the total amount of money you owe to other parties. For a company, it includes both current and long-term liabilities. It's like all the money you owe on your credit card, your mortgage, your car loan, etc. Understanding a company's debt is like knowing how much someone owes on their credit card versus how much they have in savings. A healthy balance is having more assets (savings) than liabilities (debts). For companies, this balance is shown on the balance sheet, with assets on one side and how they're financed (equity and debt) on the other.

A simple way to gauge a company's financial health is by looking at its debt-to-equity ratio, which compares what it owes to what it owns. For example, if a company has $18 billion in equity and $1.7 billion in debt, its balance sheet is strong, showing it's more financed by ownership than by debt. This ratio matters because, in tough times, companies with less debt are more likely to survive.

High debt can be risky, especially bank debt, which might need to be paid back suddenly. Funded debt, like long-term corporate bonds, is less risky because it doesn't have to be repaid immediately. This gives companies room to manoeuvre and time to recover from short-term setbacks.

Looking at debt structures helped investors believe in companies like Chrysler during its financial struggles because, despite its debts, it had a significant cash reserve and a manageable loan arrangement that signalled it wasn't going under anytime soon. Similarly, Micron Technology's ability to convert its bank debt into a long-term convertible debenture allowed it to survive and eventually thrive once the market for its products improved.

In essence, while debt can signal danger, understanding its structure and how it compares to a company's equity can reveal opportunities for informed investors.

8. **Interest expenses:** These are the costs incurred due to borrowed money. It's like the interest you pay on your credit card balance or a home loan.

9. **Net sales:** This represents the total revenue that a company generates from its business operations after deductions such as returns, allowances and discounts. In a simple comparison, imagine you have a garage sale and sell goods worth $100, but you give discounts worth $10 and accept returns worth $5, then your net sales will be $85.

10. **Cost of goods sold (COGS):** This is the direct costs related to producing the goods sold by a company. It includes the cost of materials and direct labour costs. In everyday life, if you bake and sell cakes, the cost of flour, eggs, sugar, etc., and the cost of baking are the COGS.

11. **Net credit sales:** These are the sales made by a business where payment is not received at the time of transaction. Imagine selling a piece of furniture, and the buyer promises to pay you later; this is a credit sale.

12. **Average total assets:** This is the average value of the things you own (assets) during a specific period. It is calculated by adding the asset value at the beginning of the period to the asset value at the end, then dividing by 2.

13. **Accounts payable:** This is the money a company owes its suppliers or vendors for goods or services received but not yet paid for. It's like the bill you receive for utilities or credit card charges which you have to pay in the future.

14. **Accounts receivable:** This is money that is owed to a company by its customers for goods or services that have been delivered but not yet paid for. If you lend a friend $10, that's an account receivable until your friend pays you back.

15. **Gross profit:** This is the total sales minus the cost of goods sold. If you sell a painting for $100 and the cost to create that painting (canvas, paint, brushes, etc.) is $30, your gross profit would be $70.

16. **Operating income:** This is the income generated from the main business operations, which is calculated by subtracting operating expenses (like rent, salaries, utilities, etc.) from gross profit.

17. **Net profit:** This is the profit left over after all expenses (including taxes and interest) have been subtracted from the revenue. This is the bottom line or the actual profit that the business or person makes.

18. **Net income:** Similar to net profit, it is the income remaining after all costs, expenses and taxes have been deducted from revenue.

19. **Total investment:** This is the sum of all the money invested. If you put $1000 in stocks, $2000 in bonds and $5000 in a savings account, your total investment would be $8000.

20. **Invested capital:** This refers to the total amount of money that has been invested into a business. In a personal setting, this might be similar to the money you've put into improving your home, such as the costs of renovations and upgrades.

21. **Market capitalization:** This is the total value of all a company's shares of stock. It's calculated by multiplying the company's share price by the total number of its outstanding shares. It would be like the total value of your cookie business if you were to price each cookie and multiply it by the total number of cookies you have.

22. **Free cash flow (FCF):** This is the cash a company generates after accounting for cash outflows to support operations and maintain its capital assets. In personal finance, it would be similar to the money left over after you've paid all your bills and set aside money for future necessary expenses, like home or car maintenance.

Cash flow is essentially how much money a company has coming in from its business activities. Imagine a lemonade stand; for every cup sold, that's cash coming in. But, to keep selling, you might need to buy more lemons and sugar, which is cash going out. A business like Philip

Morris, which sells products without needing constant, expensive updates (like a new lemonade stand or fancier cups), keeps more of the cash it makes. This is easier and more profitable than a business that has to continually invest in expensive equipment just to keep up, like a steel company.

A simple way to look at it is through the lens of a $20 stock. If it brings in $2 per share in cash flow annually, that's a decent 10% return. However, if you find one bringing in $10 per share, that's an incredible deal, suggesting you might want to invest heavily.

The key is to focus on 'free cash flow', which is what's left after covering all those necessary expenses to keep the business running. It's the money a company can use freely, whether to reinvest, pay dividends, or buy back shares. For instance, Coastal Corporation looked average on paper, but it had a lot of free cash flow thanks to minimal upkeep costs on its pipeline investments, making it a hidden gem for investors.

In essence, companies with high free cash flow, especially those with low maintenance costs, can be great investment opportunities. They have more flexibility to reward shareholders and invest in growth, making them potentially less risky and more rewarding investments.

23. **Annual EPS growth:** EPS stands for Earnings Per Share. This is the portion of a company's profit allocated to each outstanding share of common stock. The growth of this over a year is the annual EPS growth. You do not need to understand it, just that the more it grows, the better.

Financial Metrics to Gauge Company's Financial Strength

1. Liquidity Ratios

'Liquidity' is the company's ability to convert assets into cash so that it can pay its short-term debts. 'Solvency' is the long-term capability of the company to generate money consistently. Thus, liquidity ratios are used to measure the company's ability to meet short-term or current liabilities. Let's imagine you're planning a road trip. You need to know if your car has enough gas to reach the next gas station. In this scenario, the gas in your car represents your 'current assets,' and the distance to the next station represents your 'current liabilities.' The more gas you have relative to the distance, the better.

The liquidity ratios differ from solvency as liquidity deals with the working capital performance, whereas solvency deals with the company's effectiveness in paying all its debts and liabilities. The common liquidity ratios are the current ratio, quick ratio, and cash ratio.

a. Current Ratio

Formula: Current Assets/Current Liabilities

The current ratio measures a company's ability to pay its current liabilities with its current assets. A ratio of 1:1 is considered ideal. Current ratio is like comparing the amount of money you have in your pocket (current assets) to the cost of items in your shopping cart (current liabilities). The current ratio ascertains how the current assets of the companies, such as cash and cash equivalents, inventories and accounts receivable, are used to pay off current and short-term liabilities, such as accounts payable. Therefore, a high current ratio indicates sufficient liquidity to meet short-term debts.

Let's look at an example of a company and calculate its current ratio. Apple Inc. (AAPL) reported its current assets and current liabilities as of September 30th, 2022, as stated in its annual balance sheet:

Cash On Hand = $48,304 (number in millions of dollars)
Receivables = $60,932
Inventory = $4,946
Other Current Assets = $21,223
Total Current Liabilities = $153,982

Hence, in this case, its

Current Assets =
$48,304+$60,932+$4,946+$21,223 = $135,405

and Current Ratio = $135,405/$153,982 = 0.8794.

The above current ratio of 0.88 implies that if Apple were to convert all its short-term assets into liquid funds, it would only be able to cover 88% of its short-term debt.

b. **Quick Ratio**

Formula:
(Current Assets − Inventories − Prepaid Expenses) / Current Liabilities

The quick ratio is a more stringent measure of a company's liquidity, as it only includes highly liquid assets in the calculation. The quick ratio is like the current ratio but it removes items that aren't so easy to convert to cash (inventories and prepaid expenses). It's like counting only cash and ignoring the value of the gift cards in your wallet. Thus, the quick ratio, or the acid-test ratio, measures how much of the company's most liquid assets, such as cash and cash equivalents and accounts receivable, are available to meet the current liabilities. Usually, the industry average for the quick ratio is 1. It excludes inventories from the calculation as those are not readily convertible into cash. Taking the above example of AAPL, we can calculate its quick ratio.

Its quick ratio as of September 30th, 2022
= Current Assets-Inventories/Current Liabilities
= $(135,405-$4,946)/$153,982
= $130,459/$153,982=0.85.

c. **Cash Ratio**

Formula: Cash and cash equivalents/Current Liabilities

This is the most conservative liquidity measure. It's like checking if you can pay your shopping bill just with the cash in your pocket without resorting to credit cards or gift cards. Thus, the cash ratio is the measure of a company's ability to use its cash and cash equivalents to settle its short-term or current obligations. The higher the ratio, the higher the company's ability to quickly pay off its current liabilities using its most liquid current assets, i.e., cash and cash equivalents.

2. **Leverage Ratios**

You must be familiar with the concept of leverage, as some brokers provide such a facility. For example, if you have 1,000 euros and want to buy a stock worth 2,000 euros, the broker allows a leverage of 2:1. This means that your 1,000 euros enables you to purchase the 2,000-euro stock; however, if the stock's value goes up or down by 10%, the impact on your capital will be 20%.

These ratios tell us how much debt a company has relative to its assets or equity. Think about buying a house. The amount of mortgage you have on the house relative to its total value of your equity in it gives you a sense of your financial risk.

Companies use financial debt for their operations. So, it becomes important to understand the company's financial health to meet its debt obligations. Hence, calculating leverage ratios becomes essential to ascertain the company's ability to manage its financial risk. The leverage ratios that are commonly used are:

a. **Debt-to-Equity Ratio (D/E Ratio)**

   Formula: Total Debt/Total Equity

   The D/E ratio is the proportion of a company's financing that comes from debt versus equity. A high ratio may indicate that a company is taking on too much debt. The D/E ratio is like comparing the amount you owe on your mortgage (total debt) to the part of the house you truly own (total equity). It is a measure of a company's financial leverage and is calculated by dividing the company's overall debt by its shareholders' equity. A high D/E ratio may indicate that a company is heavily leveraged, while a low D/E ratio may indicate that a company has a strong financial position. However, it's important to note that different industries have different debt-to-equity ratios, so it's essential to compare a company's ratio with its industry average to get a better idea of its financial health.

b. Debt-to-Assets Ratio (D/A Ratio)

Formula: Total Debt/Total Assets

The D/ ratio is the proportion of a company's assets that are financed through debt. A high ratio may indicate that a company is taking on too much debt. The D/A ratio is like comparing the amount you owe on your mortgage (total debt) to the total value of your house (total assets). It measures the company's debt in relation to its total assets. The ratio's high value indicates the company's higher leverage which increases the financial risk.

c. Interest Coverage Ratio

Formula: EBIT/Interest expenses

This is like checking if your salary (EBIT) is sufficient to cover your monthly interest payment (interest expenses). The interest coverage ratio measures a company's efficiency in paying the interest on its debt. It's calculated by dividing a company's earnings before interest and taxes (EBIT) by its incurred interest expenses. If the ratio is high, the company can easily pay its interest expenses, which is a good sign. On the other hand, if the ratio is low, it could indicate that the company may struggle to pay its interest expenses.

It is also important to understand the reference values for high and low. A ratio of less than one is bad, and greater than one is good, and you can compare the obtained value with the company with the highest market capitalization in the same industry. Why is this important? Well, because if you get a value of 0.85 but see that the industry average is 0.6 due to the nature of the industry, a 0.85 value would be excellent.

3. Efficiency Ratios

Efficiency ratios are the financial metrics to gauge how well a company uses its working capital to generate revenue. Consider a factory. How many products does it produce in a day? How fast does it sell its stock? These ratios provide the operational effectiveness of the company. The commonly used efficiency ratios to gauge the operational efficiency of the company are:

a. Asset Turnover Ratio

Formula: Net sales/Average total assets

This measures a company's ability to generate revenue from its assets. A higher ratio indicates more efficient use of assets. Asset turnover ratio is a financial metric that evaluates the company's ability to effectively generate sales from its assets. It's like the number of Uber rides a driver can provide (net sales) with his car (total assets) in a day.

A higher asset turnover ratio indicates better efficiency of the company in generating revenue by utilizing its assets. In contrast, a lower ratio indicates inefficiency in utilizing the assets to generate revenue. It may vary from one industry to another, so it becomes important to compare the company's ratio with those in the same industry.

b. Inventory Turnover Ratio

Formula: Cost of goods sold/Average value of inventory

The inventory turnover ratio measures the speed at which a company sells its inventory and replenishes it over a specific period. It's like how quickly a supermarket sells its stock (cost of goods sold) compared to the average amount of stock it carries (inventory).

A high inventory turnover indicates that the company can generate cash flow quickly by selling its inventory, and the risk of obsolete inventory is reduced. On the other hand, a lower ratio indicates higher holding-up costs for inventory related to its storing and handling, leading to cash constraints. The ratio is different for different industries; thus, it is only reasonable to compare the company's ratio with its peers in the same industry.

c. **Days Sales in Inventory Ratio**

   Formula: Inventory / Cost of goods sold x (no. of days in the period)

   This ratio calculates how long the business holds the inventory before it is converted to finished goods or sold to the customer. Holding inventory for too long is not recommended because it leads to higher storage and managing inventory costs.

d. **Payable Turnover Ratio**

   Formula: Cost of Goods sold (or net credit purchases) / Average Accounts Payable

   The payable turnover ratio is a financial ratio that measures how quickly the company pays off its vendors and creditors. A higher ratio indicates the company pays off its suppliers quickly and can negotiate payment terms based on good relationships, whereas a low ratio indicates the payment is delayed and can lead to a strained relationship with the vendors and harm the company's creditworthiness.

e. **Days Payable Outstanding Ratio (DPO)**

   Formula: (Average Accounts Payable / Cost of Goods Sold) x Number of Days in Accounting Period (or year)

   This ratio indicates the number of days a company takes to pay off its suppliers. A lower ratio may indicate that the company is not taking advantage of longer credit payment terms and letting go of cash quickly. In contrast, a higher DPO indicates the company takes longer to pay off its suppliers, which can result in disputes.

f. **Receivables Turnover Ratio**

   Formula: Net credit sales/Average accounts receivable

   The payable turnover ratio is a financial ratio that measures how quickly the company collects payments from its credit customers. A higher ratio indicates that the company can generate cash flow quickly by collecting payment from its customers soon, thereby reducing the risk of receivables turning into bad debts. In contrast, a lower ratio indicates the company takes too long to collect payments from its credit customers, which can lead to cash constraints.

   The ratio of receivables turnover varies from industry to industry; hence, a high ratio in one industry may be considered low in another. Therefore, it's important to compare the companies within the same industry.

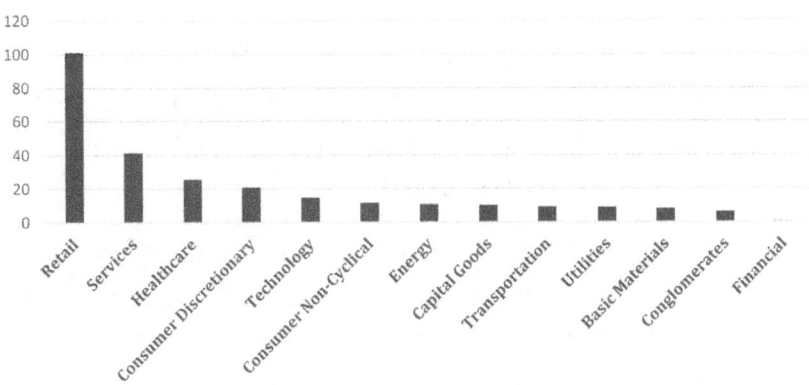

Data Source: https://csimarket.com/screening/index.php?s=rt&pageS=1&fis=

None of the efficiency ratios should be used in isolation to determine a company's ability to generate cash flows. Rather, the combination of different ratios helps to understand a company's policies and efficiency to generate consistent cash flows.

4. Profitability Ratios

Profitability ratios are the financial metrics used to ascertain a company's ability to generate profits using the available resources. Think of your salary: How much do you make before and after taxes? What portion of your income do you save?

Though a higher ratio is advisable, it is important to compare the same with the company's historical performance and that of its peers in the same industry. Some of the profitability ratios that are used are:

a. **Gross Margin**

   Formula: Gross profit/Net sales

   The gross margin is calculated by dividing a company's gross profit by its total revenue. It's like the proportion of your salary (gross profit) left after subtracting the cost of your commute (net sales).

   Gross profit is the amount of money a company makes from its core business operations after accounting for the cost of goods sold. Total revenue is the total amount of money a company brings from its business operations.

b. **Operating Margin**

   Formula: Operating income/Net sales

   The operating margin is calculated by dividing a company's operating income by its total revenue. It's the portion of your salary (operating income) remaining after paying all your monthly bills (net sales).

   Operating income is the amount of money a company makes from its core business operations after accounting for both the cost of goods sold and its operating expenses.

c. **Net Profit Margin**

   Formula: Net profit/Revenue

   This is the portion of your income (net profit) you can save after all your monthly expenses have been paid. Thus, net profit margin is a measure of a company's profitability after accounting for all of its expenses, including taxes and interest. It is calculated by dividing a company's net income by its total revenue. Net income is the amount of money a company makes after accounting for all of its expenses, including the cost of goods sold, operating expenses, taxes and interest. Total revenue is the total amount of money a company brings in from its business operations.

In general, a higher margin indicates that a company is more profitable. However, it's important to compare a company's margins to those of its competitors and the industry average to get a complete picture of its profitability. Additionally, it's important to consider other factors, such as a company's growth potential and financial health, when making investment decisions.

d. **Return on Assets (ROA)**

Formula: Net income/Total assets

The ROA ratio measures a company's efficiency in using its assets to generate profit. Therefore, a higher ROA indicates that a company uses its assets more effectively to generate profits.

e. **Return on Equity (ROE)**

Formula: Net income/Total equity

The return on equity (ROE) is a measure of a company's profitability concerning its shareholders' equity. It is calculated by dividing the company's net income by its shareholders' equity. A high ROE may indicate that a company is generating strong profits for its shareholders, while a low ROE may indicate that a company is struggling to generate profits.

f. **Return on Investment (ROI) and Return on Invested Capital (ROIC)**

Formula: ROI= Profit/Total investment and ROIC= Profit/Invested capital

These ratios may not be as widely known or easily accessible as some of the others we've discussed. They are powerful tools for investors looking to gauge a company's financial health and long-term potential. This is like comparing the profit you make from selling a house (profit) to the price you paid for the house (total investment or invested capital). The higher the ratio, the better the investment.

ROI stands for return on investment and is a financial metric that measures an investment's efficiency. It is expressed as a percentage and calculated by dividing the profit of an investment by the total cost of the investment.

ROIC, on the other hand, stands for return on invested capital and is a similar metric, but it considers the amount of capital invested into a business.

Investors often use these metrics to determine how effectively a company uses its capital to generate profits. Let's use an example to explain the difference between the two metrics. Let's say that you invest $2 million in a business and take out a $3 million loan. At the end of the year, the business generates a profit of $10 million. To calculate the ROI, you would divide the profit ($10 million) by the total investment ($2 million + $3 million = $5 million), giving you an ROI of 100%.

ROI = (Profit/Total investment) x 100 ROI = ($10 million/$5 million) x 100 ROI = 200%

To calculate the ROIC, you would divide the profit ($10 million) by the invested capital ($2 million), which gives you an ROIC of 400%.

ROIC = (Profit/Invested capital) x 100 ROIC = ($10 million/$2 million) x 100 ROIC = 500%

As you can see, the ROIC is much higher than the ROI. This is because the ROIC only considers the capital invested into the business, while the ROI includes the loan taken out. However, it's important to note that the ROIC can be a more conservative measure of profitability, as it doesn't consider the cost of debt. You may use one metric or the other depending on your investment strategy.

Thus, while calculating ROI and ROIC, we need to consider the quality of the debt. We can determine this by looking at the debt-to-equity ratio and interest coverage ratio. Moreover, we can check if the company can pay its debt by looking at the cash flow statement. By taking these factors into account, we can make better-informed investment decisions.

5. Market Value Ratios

Market value ratios are financial tools or metrics to measure the value of a company's share. Consider a house for sale: Is the price fair? How does it compare to its intrinsic value?

Investors use such ratios to ascertain the share value of a company. The ratios are used in combination with other financial metrics by the investors to arrive at their investment decisions. The commonly used market value ratios are:

a. **Price-earnings ratio (P/E)**

Formula: Share price/Earnings per share

The P/E ratio is a popular ratio used to evaluate a company's stock price. It's like comparing the price of a house (share price) to the rent it could earn in a year (earnings per share).

The P/E ratio divides the current stock price by the company's earnings per share (EPS). A higher P/E ratio indicates that investors are willing to pay more for each dollar of earnings, which can be a sign of confidence in the company's future growth prospects.

A company's lower P/E ratio than the industry may indicate that the company is undervalued. Moreover, if the current P/E ratio is lower than its historical average, it could indicate that the company is in a good position to appreciate its value in the future.

The essence of every intelligent form of investing is to buy stocks for less than what they're worth. The valuation of a company shows you how much the market is willing to pay for a certain stock. There are many different methods to look at a company's valuation. The most used valuation metric is the price-earnings ratio (P/E) ratio.

You can calculate it as follows:

Price-earnings ratio = stock price/earnings per share
Let's take S&P Global (a wide moat stock) as an example.

S&P Global currently trades at a stock price of $360 while its earnings per share for 2023 are expected to be equal to $11.07.

As a result, S&P Global's P/E is equal to 32.5.

The lower the P/E ratio, the cheaper the stock. When you divide the earnings per share of a company by its stock price, you get the earnings yield:

Earnings yield = earnings per share/stock price S&P

Global's earnings yield is equal to 3.1% ($11.07/$360).

This means that when you would buy S&P Global for $10.000 today, the company would generate $310 (3.1%) in earnings for you next year.

b. **Price-to-book (P/B) ratio**

Formula: Market price per share/Book value per share

or

Market Capitalization/Total book value

The price-to-book ratio (P/B ratio) is a measure of a company's current share price relative to its book value per share. This is like comparing the market price of a house (market price per share) to the price it was bought for originally (book value per share). It is calculated by dividing the company's current share price by its book value per share.

Investors use this ratio to interpret the market's perception of the company's share value. A higher ratio indicates increased confidence of the market participants in the company's future growth potential. Moreover, it also indicates how much the equity investors pay for each dollar in the company's net assets. A low ratio of less than one usually indicates the company is undervalued, and a ratio of greater than 1 indicates the company is overvalued. Since the ratio differs among companies in different sectors, comparing companies within the same sector is better.

For example, let's say a company has 2 million in equity and a market capitalization of 1 million. Its P/B ratio would be 0.5 (1/2), indicating that the company is being valued at a 50% discount to its book value.

c. **Dividend Yield**

Formula: Dividend per share/Share price

Imagine investing in a business and receiving a share of the profit every year. The dividend yield is like the profit you receive from that business each year (dividend per share) compared to the price you paid to invest in the business (share price). Thus, it is the proportion of a company's earnings that are paid out as dividends to its shareholders. You can use the dividend yield filter to find stocks with a high dividend yield, which indicates that the company is paying out a large portion of its earnings as dividends.

d. **Price-to-sales (P/S) ratio**

Formula: Share price/Sales per share

The price-to-sales ratio (P/S ratio) is a measure of a company's current share price relative to its sales per share. It's like comparing the price of a restaurant (share price) to its annual food sales (sales per share).

The P/S ratio is calculated by dividing the company's current share price by its sales per share. A high P/S ratio may indicate that a company's shares are overvalued, while a low P/S ratio may indicate that a company's shares are undervalued.

e. **P/FCF (Price to Free Cash Flow)**

Formula: Market capitalization/Free cash flow

P/FCF is another ratio that investors use widely. This is like comparing the price of a business (market capitalization) to its leftover money after all expenses, reinvestments, and debt repayments (free cash flow).

Free cash flow is the cash a company generates after accounting for capital expenditures (money spent on maintaining or expanding the business). This ratio is important because it helps investors determine how efficiently a company generates cash.

To calculate P/FCF, you can simply divide the market capitalization by the free cash flow. Like P/E, a lower P/FCF ratio suggests that the company is undervalued. However, unlike P/E, P/FCF uses cash flow instead of earnings, which some consider a more reliable indicator of a company's financial health. Furthermore, free cash flow is important because it can be used to pay dividends, reduce debt, or reinvest in the business.

Companies with high free cash flow are better positioned to weather economic downturns or make strategic investments. As with other ratios, it's important to compare a company's P/FCF ratio to those of its peers in the same industry or sector. A lower P/FCF ratio than the company's industry average or historical average may indicate that the company is undervalued.

While P/E is a widely used ratio, P/FCF is becoming increasingly popular among investors due to its emphasis on cash flow, often viewed as a more reliable indicator of a company's financial health.

f. **PEG ratio**

    Formula: (P/E ratio)/Annual EPS growth

    The PEG ratio measures a company's growth potential concerning its price-to-earnings ratio (P/E ratio). This is like comparing the price you pay for a house (P/E ratio) to how fast its value is increasing (annual EPS growth). A low PEG could mean you're getting a bargain for a rapidly appreciating house, while a high PEG could mean you're overpaying for a house that's not appreciating quickly. It is calculated by dividing the company's P/E ratio by its expected earnings growth rate.

Now that you have understood the various financial metrics you can use to gauge a company's financial health, it is important to remember that no particular ratio should be used in isolation. Rather, the financial ratios should be used in combination with other parameters to make investing decisions. Warren Buffett, in his letter to the shareholders in 2000, stated:

'Common yardsticks such as dividend yield, the ratio of price to earnings or to book value, and even growth rates have nothing to do with valuation except to the extent they provide clues to the amount and timing of cash flows into and from the business. Indeed, growth can destroy value if it requires cash inputs in the early years of a project or enterprise that exceed the discounted value of the cash that those assets will generate in later years.

Market commentators and investment managers who glibly refer to "growth" and "value" styles as contrasting approaches to investment are displaying their ignorance, not their sophistication. Growth is simply a component — usually a plus, sometimes a minus— in the value equation!'

Thus, it is quite clear that financial ratios cannot be the sole criteria for making investment decisions. Instead, investment decisions require a comprehensive approach. We will talk more about growth and value investing in detail in Chapter 7, and by the end of this book, you will be in a position to start your investing journey confidently.

When evaluating a company's financial health, looking at just the last year's figures isn't enough to get the full picture. That's like judging a movie based on its final scene without considering the entire storyline! To better understand a company's financial trends, you can use the quadratic mean (also known as the root mean square) for past years' data. This method will give you a more comprehensive view of the company's performance over time, particularly for key metrics like earnings growth and debt levels.

Here's a simplified way to calculate the quadratic mean for a company's earnings growth over three years:

We want to calculate the growth rate for each year. Suppose the earnings growth rates for the past three years are 5%, 10% and 15%.

1. **Square the annual figures:** If the growth rates or changes you're interested in for three years are, for example, 5%, 10% and 15%, first square these

numbers. That would be 25 (5^2), 100 (10^2) and 225 (15^2).

2. **Calculate the average:** Add the squared numbers (25 + 100 + 225 = 350) and then divide by 3 (the number of years). So, you'd get 350/3 = 116.67.

3. **Take the square root of the average:** Finally, find the square root of this average. The square root of 116.67 is approximately 10.8%.

This is your quadratic mean, providing a smoothed average growth rate that factors in the volatility over the period.

Applying the quadratic mean helps highlight consistent growth patterns or improvements in financial health, such as reducing debt. For example, if a company's debt reduction rates over three years are 2%, 4% and 6%, following the same steps will show a smooth improvement in reducing debt, reflecting a positive trend.

However, numbers don't always tell the whole story. It's crucial to understand the reasons behind these changes. For instance, a sudden jump in earnings could be due to a one-time sale of assets rather than operational success, which could be misleading if you're looking for sustainable growth. Similarly, a reduction in debt might look good on paper, but if it's achieved by sacrificing important investments in the company's future, it could spell trouble down the line.

Now you can pick a company you're interested in and try to find answers to the below questions to test your ability to analyse various financial ratios.

Financial Metrics to Gauge Company's Financial Strength

- What do the financial metrics tell you about its financial strength?
- Can you ascertain the company's liquidity position?
- What do the various profitability ratios of the company reveal?
- How far is the company efficiently utilizing its assets to generate revenue?

CHAPTER 6
CORPORATE GOVERNANCE PRACTICES - WHY ARE THEY IMPORTANT FOR INVESTING?

"Plans are useless,
but planning is indispensable."

– Dwight D. Eisenhower

What do you think are the most important benefits of good corporate governance for a company? How can investors effectively assess a company's corporate governance practices before making investment decisions? This chapter deals with corporate governance, and by the end of it, you will have your answers to these questions.

The interests of many stakeholders, such as shareholders, suppliers, customers, vendors, government and even society as a whole, are involved with the functioning of the company. Hence, it becomes indispensable that the company functions in an accountable, fair, and transparent manner.

Corporate governance provides a structural framework setting out the policies and rules for the company to follow to achieve its objectives. The company's board of directors is tasked with important corporate decisions and directly influences corporate governance.

In the tapestry of corporate governance, family-owned businesses stand out with a unique thread of continuity and commitment that often translates into superior performance. This graph, sourced from Credit Suisse Research and Thomson Reuters Datastream, illustrates a compelling narrative: over time, family-owned businesses have not just held their own, but have frequently outpaced their non-family counterparts in the marketplace. It suggests that the stewardship associated with family ownership can lead to a focused vision and strategy, driving consistent value creation over the long term.

FAMILY OWNED BUSINESSES TEND TO OUTPERFORM

Figure 4: Market-capitalization-weighted and sector-adjusted returns – family-owned alpha through time

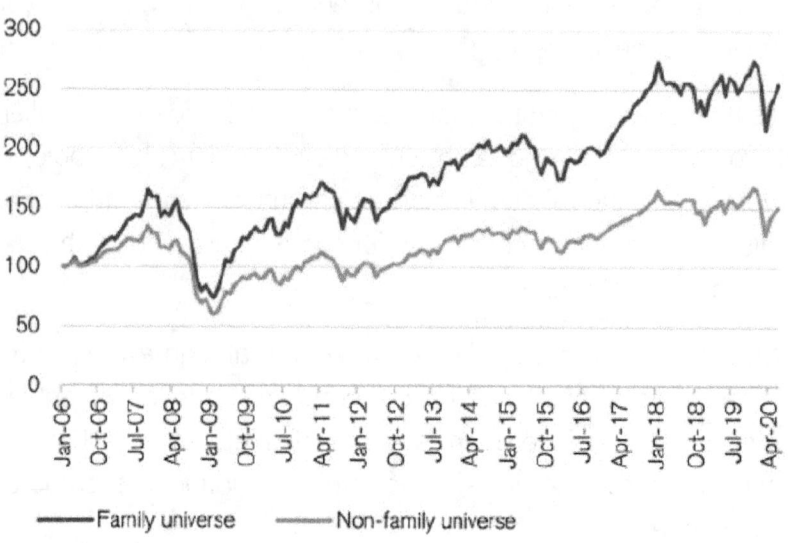

Source Figures 3–4: Credit Suisse Research, Thomson Reuters Datastream

Image Credit: Credit Suisse

↗ Understanding Corporate Governance and Its Benefits

The board is primarily responsible for governance. It must understand that it's not enough for a company to be merely profitable. Companies must also display good corporate citizenship. This is achieved through ethical behaviour and a strong commitment to environmental sustainability.

- Sound corporate governance benefits companies in numerous ways.

- It builds trust and confidence among public officials, the community, and investors. This is because transparency in operations and financial matters assures stakeholders that the company is run ethically and responsibly.

- Responsible corporate governance gives stakeholders and investors a clear understanding of the company's plans and integrity. This is achieved through regular communication of the company's objectives, strategies, and progress toward its goals. Transparency in these areas reassures stakeholders of the company's commitment to its stated objectives.

- Good corporate governance also promotes financial viability and opportunity in the long run. By following sound business practices and maintaining a strong ethical stance, companies can attract long-term investment and support, which contributes to their financial stability.

↗ Principles of Corporate Governance

The commonly known principles of corporate governance are as follows:

Transparency
The board should provide accurate and transparent information about conflicts of interest and financial performance. It should also indicate matters that can be potentially risky to the stakeholders.

Fairness
The board must treat employees, vendors, communities and shareholders fairly with equal consideration.

Risk Management
The board and the management must determine all kinds of risks and take measures to control them. Moreover, the

existence and status of the risks should be communicated to the relevant parties.

Responsibility and Accountability
The board is responsible for all corporate matters. It must act in the best interest of the company and its stakeholders. It is also accountable for the company's overall performance and should communicate important issues to the shareholders.

Assessment of Corporate Governance- Making the Assessment Process Actionable

The assessment of a company's corporate governance can feel like an intimidating task, especially for individual investors. However, it is a crucial step in making informed investment decisions. Here are more specific steps and resources investors can use to effectively carry out these assessments:

Reviewing the Company's Governance Structure
The company's annual reports, proxy statements, and other official documents usually contain detailed information about its board of directors and any committees in place. Websites like Yahoo Finance, Google Finance, or the company's own investor relations page often provide these documents.

Assessing Board Independence
You can usually find details about the board's independence in the company's proxy statement. This document also provides information about the directors' backgrounds, their affiliation with the company, and their holdings in the company.

Reviewing Executive Compensation Policies
Details about executive compensation are also typically found in the company's proxy statement. Websites such as Glassdoor and PayScale can provide some insight into the

company's broader compensation practices and help identify any disproportionate compensation at the top.

Assessing Risk Management Practices

While detailed risk management information might not be publicly available, the company's annual report often provides insight into the major risks facing the company and the steps it is taking to manage those risks.

Reviewing Financial Statements and Disclosures

The company's quarterly reports (10-Q), and annual reports are key documents to review here. These documents are publicly available on the U.S. Securities and Exchange Commission's EDGAR database or on the respective stock exchange's website, where the company is listed.

An annual report is a document that companies publish each year to provide shareholders and the public with an overview of their financial performance, operations, and strategies. It typically includes highlights from the year, financial statements, management's discussion and analysis, and other relevant information. On the other hand, a 10-K report is a more detailed and comprehensive filing required by the Securities and Exchange Commission (SEC) for publicly traded companies. It contains in-depth financial information, risk factors, legal proceedings, management structure, and other essential details about the company's operations and performance. In this chapter, to keep things simple, we'll use them interchangeably.

Let's take an example to understand how to review 10-K. The below screenshot is the 10-K form of First Republic Bank for the year 2022, which you can find on the FDIC website.

Book Value per Common Share and Tangible Book Value per Common Share [1]	December 31, 2022	2021
(in millions, except per share amounts)		
Total shareholders' equity	$17,446	$15,898
Less: Preferred stock	(3,633)	(3,633)
Total common shareholders' equity (a)	13,813	12,265
Less: Goodwill and other intangible assets	(218)	(222)
Total tangible common shareholders' equity (b)	$13,595	$12,043
Number of shares of common stock outstanding (c)	183	179
Book value per common share (a) / (c)	$ 75.38	$ 68.34
Tangible book value per common share (b) / (c)	$ 74.19	$ 67.10

[1] Tangible book value per common share is considered a non-GAAP financial measure, and is reconciled to GAAP book value per common share in this table.

The banks that had significantly negative tangible mark-to-market equity have already gone under. First Republic (FRC) is a great example of this. They had reported $13.6B ($74/share) of tangible book value for the year ended 2022.

($ in millions)	Carrying Value	Fair Value Total	Level 1	Level 2	Level 3
Assets:					
Cash and cash equivalents	$ 4,283	$ 4,283	$4,283	$ —	$ —
Debt securities held-to-maturity, net: [1]					
U.S. Government-sponsored agency securities	165	138	—	138	—
Agency residential MBS	2,003	1,753	—	1,753	—
Other residential MBS	8	7	—	7	—
Agency commercial MBS	5,331	4,663	—	4,663	—
Securities of U.S. states and political subdivisions:					
Tax-exempt municipal securities	17,635	14,765	—	14,743	22
Tax-exempt nonprofit debentures	69	69	—	—	69
Taxable municipal securities	1,725	1,235	—	1,235	—
Corporate debt securities	1,412	957	—	957	—
Loans, net: [1]					
Real estate secured mortgages	136,793	117,520	—	84,347	33,173
Other loans	29,291	26,405	—	—	26,405
Other assets:					
MSRs	11	26	—	—	26
FHLB stock	379	379	—	—	379
Liabilities:					
Deposits:					
CDs	$ 25,212	$ 25,202	$ —	$ —	$25,202
Short-term FHLB advances	6,700	6,704	—	6,704	—
Long-term FHLB advances	7,300	7,050	—	7,050	—
Senior notes	500	498	—	498	—
Subordinated notes	779	621	—	621	—

[1] Carrying value is presented net of ACL.

The banks do not have to market a loan book because they only would do so during irrational fear that causes them to panic sell their loans in a desperate rush for liquidity. Well, rightly or wrongly, FRC got hit with fear and a run, and their loan book proved a huge problem.

Checking Regulatory Compliance
Investors can check a company's regulatory filings for any violations or fines. Additionally, news articles and business news websites can provide up-to-date information about any regulatory issues facing the company.

Looking for Stakeholder Engagement
Evidence of stakeholder engagement can often be found in the company's sustainability or corporate social responsibility report. These reports are usually available on the company's website.

By following these steps, investors can gain a thorough understanding of a company's corporate governance practices and make more informed investment decisions.

Corporate Governance Models

Businesses worldwide may have common objectives, but companies' corporate structures vary substantially. Thus, there are broadly three corporate governance models, each with its own set of practices.

Anglo-American Model
The Anglo-American corporate governance model is the most common in countries such as the United States and the United Kingdom. This model is characterized by a shareholder-centered approach to corporate governance where the board of directors is responsible for representing shareholders' interests. The board typically comprises independent directors not affiliated with the company or its management and is accountable to shareholders.

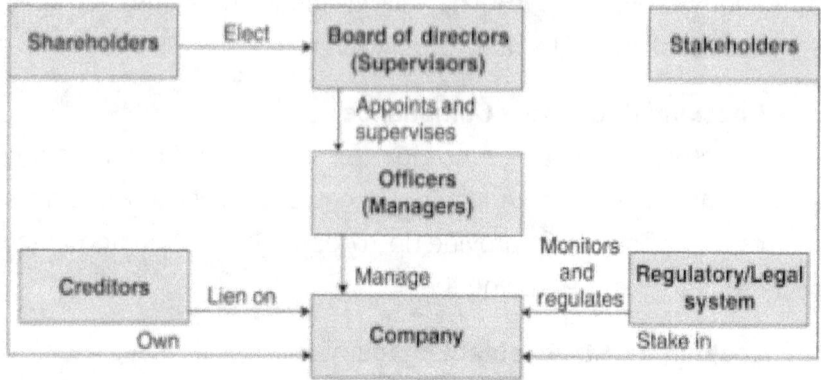

Source: https://www.oreilly.com/library/view/business-ethics-and/9789332511255/xhtml/c14s11.xhtml

Under the Anglo-American model, companies prioritize maximizing shareholder value, often through aggressive growth strategies and cost-cutting measures. As a result, it can lead to short-term thinking and neglect of other stakeholders, such as employees, customers, and the environment. However, this model has been credited with promoting entrepreneurship and innovation and encouraging a competitive business environment.

The Continental Model

The continental corporate governance model is common in European countries such as Germany and France. This model is characterized by a stakeholder-centered approach, where the interests of all stakeholders – including shareholders, employees, customers and suppliers – are considered. The board of directors typically comprises representatives from each stakeholder group, with employee representatives being a key feature. There are two groups – the executive board and the supervisory council. The executive board is entrusted with corporate management, and the supervisory council chosen by shareholders and employees controls the executive board.

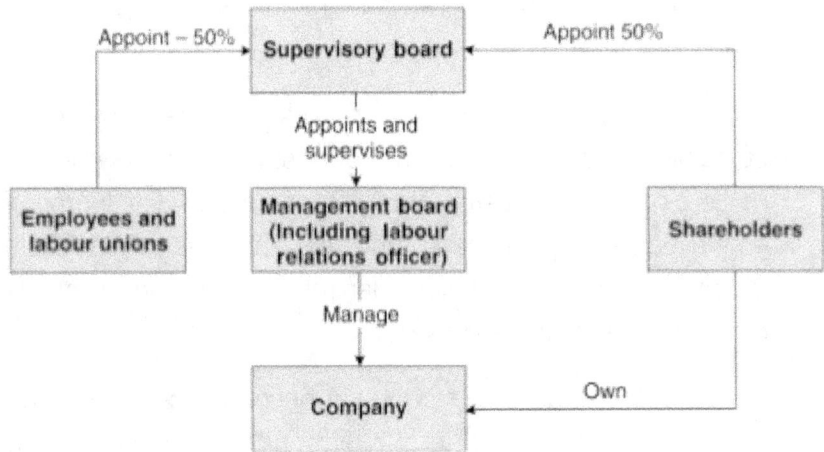

Source: https://www.oreilly.com/library/view/business-ethics-and/9789332511255/xhtml/c14s11.xhtml

Under the continental model, companies prioritize long-term sustainability over short-term profits. This can lead to a focus on investment and innovation and a more stable and predictable business environment. However, critics argue that this model can be slow to adapt to changing market conditions and is overly bureaucratic.

The Japanese Model

The Japanese corporate governance model is characterized by a close relationship between companies and their stakeholders, including employees, customers and suppliers. This model strongly emphasizes long-term relationships, trust and the importance of consensus-building and collaboration. The model includes two forms of relationships – one is between shareholders, creditors, suppliers, customers and employee unions. The other is between shareholders, managers and administrators. Further, there exists joint responsibility and balance known as keiretsu (Japanese term for a business network made up of various companies comprising supply chain partners, distributors, manufacturers and sometimes even financiers) in the Japanese model.

Under the Japanese model, companies prioritize stability and sustainability over short-term profits and are often willing to make significant investments in research and development, employee training and other long-term initiatives. As a result, it can lead to strong stakeholder relationships and a highly motivated and engaged workforce.

However, the Japanese model has been criticized for being slow to adapt to changing market conditions and for being too focused on the interests of large, established companies rather than individual investors, which compromises corporate transparency.

Overall, each model has its strengths and weaknesses, and companies must carefully consider which model best suits their specific situation and goals. Good corporate governance requires a balanced approach that considers all stakeholders' interests and prioritizes ethical and responsible practices.

Examples of Poor Corporate Governance

Unfortunately, there have been several high-profile cases of companies where corporate governance was poor and ultimately led to the revelation of fraudulent practices engaged in by the companies. Here are a few examples.

Enron Corporation

Enron Corporation was a US-based energy company that collapsed in 2001 due to a massive accounting fraud scandal. The company used unethical and illegal accounting practices to hide losses and inflate profits while senior executives enriched themselves at the expense of shareholders and employees. In addition, the board of directors failed to provide adequate oversight, and the company's auditors, Arthur Andersen, were complicit in the fraud.

Enron's stock price plummeted from a high of $90 per share in August 2000 to less than $1 per share by November 2001 following the revelation of the accounting fraud scandal. The company ultimately filed for bankruptcy in December 2001.

Volkswagen

In 2015, Volkswagen was found to have installed illegal software in its diesel cars to cheat on emissions tests. The scandal led to billions of dollars in fines and legal settlements, severely damaging the company's reputation. In addition, the company's corporate governance was criticized for failing to prevent illegal activity and for lack of transparency and accountability.

Volkswagen's share price dropped significantly in the days following the announcement of the emissions scandal in September 2015. The stock price fell from around €160 per share to around €100 per share, a drop of nearly 40%. The company's share price has since recovered somewhat but has not returned to pre-scandal levels.

Wells Fargo

In 2016, Wells Fargo was found to have opened millions of unauthorized bank accounts for its customers to meet sales targets and earn bonuses. The scandal led to a $185 million fine and a significant loss of customer trust. In addition, the company's corporate governance was criticized for failing to provide adequate oversight and for allowing a toxic sales culture to flourish.

Wells Fargo's share price dropped by around 13% in the weeks following the announcement of the unauthorized accounts scandal in September 2016. The company's stock price has since recovered but has not yet returned to pre-scandal levels.

These examples demonstrate the importance of good corporate governance and the risks of failing to prioritize ethical and responsible practices. Companies prioritizing transparency, accountability and stakeholder engagement are more likely to succeed over the long term and avoid damaging scandals and legal problems.

Lessons Learned from Corporate Governance Failures

Enron Corporation

Enron's collapse was one of the largest and most shocking corporate failures in U.S. history, prompting a significant overhaul of the regulatory landscape. The scandal led to the enactment of the Sarbanes-Oxley Act of 2002, which tightened corporate financial reporting standards and increased penalties for corporate fraud. Companies have since implemented stricter internal controls and more rigorous auditing processes to prevent such instances of fraud.

For investors, the lesson is to be wary of companies with complex financial structures that are difficult to understand or where the reported earnings rely heavily on non-operating or one-time items. Additionally, unusually close relationships between a company and its auditors could be a red flag.

Volkswagen

Following the emissions scandal, Volkswagen made several changes to its corporate governance structure. The company established a new board committee responsible for compliance and risk management and increased the independence of its quality assurance department. It also invested heavily in electric vehicles and committed to more ethical and sustainable business practices.

The key lesson for investors is the importance of scrutinizing a company's environmental, social and governance (ESG) practices. Companies with poor ESG performance may face significant financial and reputational risks.

Wells Fargo

In response to the unauthorized accounts scandal, Wells Fargo took several steps to improve its corporate governance and culture. The company eliminated sales targets for its retail banking team, which had incentivized the fraudulent behaviour. It also replaced several members of its senior leadership team and board of directors.

For investors, the Wells Fargo case underscores the importance of considering a company's corporate culture when making investment decisions. A toxic corporate culture can lead to significant reputational and financial damage.

In conclusion, these cases underline the importance of robust corporate governance structures and ethical business practices. They highlight the need for companies to prioritize transparency, accountability and stakeholder engagement and the role investors can play in encouraging such behaviour by making informed investment decisions.

Positive Examples of Corporate Governance

Microsoft Corporation

Microsoft has long been recognized for its strong corporate governance practices. The company maintains a diverse and independent board of directors that regularly reviews its governance practices to ensure they meet the highest standards of transparency and accountability. Microsoft also has strong shareholder rights, including the ability for shareholders with a significant stake in the company to nominate directors. The company has been open about its commitment to ethical business practices, environmental sustainability and social responsibility, all of which have helped to build trust with stakeholders and the public.

Nestlé

Swiss multinational food and drink processing conglomerate, Nestlé, has a well-established corporate governance structure. It has a clear separation of roles between its CEO and chairman, ensuring that no single individual has unfettered decision-making power. Nestlé also has a robust system for risk management and internal controls, with regular audits to ensure compliance. The company is known for its commitment to corporate social responsibility, with initiatives aimed at promoting sustainable agriculture, improving worker welfare, and reducing environmental impact.

Unilever

Unilever, the multinational consumer goods company, is another positive example of strong corporate governance. The company has a dual-board structure in place, with executive directors and non-executive directors maintaining a balance of power. Unilever is also known for its commitment to sustainability and has integrated sustainable business practices into its strategy at all levels. The company's Sustainable Living Plan sets out ambitious targets for reducing environmental impact and improving health and well-being.

These positive examples illustrate how good corporate governance practices can not only help companies avoid legal and reputational risks but also contribute to long-term business success. These companies have recognized that good corporate governance is not just about compliance but also about creating value for all stakeholders, including shareholders, employees, customers and the wider society.

Corporate Governance Examples of Smaller Businesses

Patagonia

Patagonia, a smaller-sized outdoor clothing company based in California, is a shining example of good corporate governance in a smaller business. The company's corporate governance structure reflects its deep commitment to environmental sustainability and social responsibility. Patagonia has taken several steps to ensure its supply chain is ethical and sustainable, including sourcing organic cotton and recycled materials and auditing its suppliers for labour standards.

Moreover, Patagonia is a Certified B Corporation, meaning it meets the highest standards of verified social and environmental performance, public transparency and legal accountability to balance profit and purpose. The company's board of directors includes representatives with environmental expertise, reflecting its mission to 'build the best product, cause no unnecessary harm, use business to inspire and implement solutions to the environmental crisis.'

Basecamp

Basecamp, a Chicago-based software company, is another example of a smaller business with strong corporate governance. Basecamp's founders have been vocal advocates of ethical business practices, transparency and work-life balance. The company has a flat organizational structure, with every employee reporting directly to the founders. This structure encourages transparency and accountability, with the founders taking personal responsibility for the company's actions. Basecamp also prides itself on being self-funded and profitable, avoiding the pressures that can come with outside investors.

These examples demonstrate that corporate governance is not just a concern for large corporations. Smaller businesses and startups also need to pay attention to their governance structures and practices, which can help them build trust with customers, employees, and other stakeholders and contribute to their long-term success.

Global Perspective

Tata Group

The Tata Group, based in India, is one of Asia's most respected conglomerates and is often hailed as a model of strong corporate governance. The group comprises over 100 independent operating companies across various industries, with operations in more than 100 countries across six continents. It is known for its ethical business practices, transparency and commitment to social responsibility.

Tata Group's corporate governance is guided by the Tata Code of Conduct, which sets out the ethical standards that all group companies and employees are expected to adhere to. The Tata Sons board, the principal investment holding company and promoter of Tata Companies, includes independent directors who are prominent individuals from business, academia and other fields, ensuring diverse perspectives.

In addition, the Tata Group has a long history of community involvement and philanthropy, with 66% of the equity of Tata Sons held by philanthropic trusts. This commitment to social responsibility is a core part of the group's corporate governance and reflects its philosophy of returning wealth to the society it serves.

Safaricom

Safaricom is a leading telecommunications company in Africa based in Kenya. It has been recognized both regionally and globally for its robust corporate governance structures and practices. Safaricom's corporate governance framework focuses on accountability, integrity, transparency and quality of service.

The company's board of directors is composed of a mix of executive, non-executive and independent directors, which ensures diverse viewpoints and minimizes conflicts of interest. Safaricom also has a comprehensive risk management framework in place, overseen by a board-level Risk Management Committee.

Safaricom is committed to sustainable business practices and corporate social responsibility. It pioneered M-Pesa, a mobile money transfer service that has transformed financial inclusion in Africa. The company also has various initiatives focused on health, education, and environmental sustainability.

These examples from India and Kenya illustrate the universal importance of corporate governance and how companies from different regions and cultures can implement effective governance structures and practices.

Relevance to Investors

Investors play a crucial role in the financial markets, and their decisions impact their own financial health and that of the overall economy. Corporate governance is a key factor that should be taken into account when making investment decisions. The scandals involving Enron, Volkswagen and Wells Fargo had devastating consequences for their investors, who suffered significant financial losses.

Enron Corporation

Enron's manipulation of financial statements misled investors into believing the company was financially healthy, leading to inflated stock prices. When the fraud was exposed, the stock price plummeted, and investors lost billions of dollars. If investors had been aware of the lax corporate governance at Enron, they might have been more cautious in their investment decisions.

Volkswagen

Similarly, Volkswagen's emissions scandal reflected a failure of corporate governance, resulting in a significant drop in its share price. Investors were left in the lurch as the company's reputation and financial health took a hit. A closer examination of the company's governance structures might have revealed a culture that allowed such fraudulent practices to occur.

Wells Fargo

In the case of Wells Fargo, the scandal around the creation of unauthorized accounts revealed a lack of internal controls and a culture that prioritized sales targets over ethical behaviour. This led to a decline in the bank's stock price and a loss of trust among its customers, which could have long-term impacts on its profitability. Investors who had closely monitored Wells Fargo's corporate governance might have been able to foresee and avoid these risks.

On the other hand, companies like Tata Group and Safaricom, which have robust corporate governance practices, have managed to earn the trust and confidence of their investors. These companies' commitment to transparency, ethical conduct and stakeholder engagement has contributed to their long-term financial success and stability, benefiting their investors.

Therefore, assessing a company's corporate governance is a critical step in the investment decision-making process. It provides insights into a company's management quality, risk management capabilities and long-term sustainability – all crucial factors that can significantly impact an investor's returns.

Update on Regulatory Changes

Corporate scandals often lead to significant shifts in regulatory frameworks and industry practices, as they expose the underlying weaknesses that need to be addressed. Understanding these changes is vital for investors and companies alike, as they highlight the evolving expectations around corporate governance.

Enron Corporation

After the Enron scandal, for instance, the U.S. Congress passed the Sarbanes-Oxley Act in 2002. This legislation introduced major changes to the regulation of corporate governance and financial practice. It emphasized the importance of auditor independence, enhanced financial disclosures and increased penalties for corporate fraud. It also introduced the requirement for management to certify the accuracy of financial statements, thereby increasing the accountability of top executives.

Volkswagen

After the Volkswagen emissions scandal, there were significant changes in the regulatory environment around vehicle emissions testing, making it more stringent and less prone to manipulation. Regulatory bodies around the world also increased their scrutiny of automakers, leading to a greater emphasis on transparency and compliance within the industry.

Wells Fargo

In the wake of the Wells Fargo scandal, U.S. regulators increased their scrutiny of sales practices within the banking industry. It also led to a renewed focus on consumer protection, with the Consumer Financial Protection Bureau playing a more active role in overseeing and regulating banking practices.

General Trends

More generally, these and other corporate scandals have led to a greater focus on corporate governance worldwide. Regulators are increasingly recognizing the importance of ethical behaviour, transparency and accountability and are introducing new guidelines and standards to promote these values. For instance, the rise of ESG (Environmental, Social and Governance) investing reflects the growing importance of corporate governance in investment decisions.

These regulatory changes highlight the dynamic nature of corporate governance and the need for companies and investors to stay updated on the latest practices and regulations. Understanding these changes can help investors make more informed decisions and companies improve their governance practices to meet evolving expectations.

↗ Listing the Veil – Recognizing Signs of Corporate Fraud

As we navigate the world of investing, it's crucial to remember that behind each stock is a company, often with a complex web of operations and financials. While this tangibility of stocks provides a sense of security, it's also important to be vigilant about the potential pitfalls. So, let's delve into the most common types of accounting fraud, how companies can obscure their actual financial status, and what you, as an investor, can do to protect yourself.

1. **Intangible Assets and Goodwill**

   Goodwill often arises in business acquisitions when the purchase price exceeds the fair value of the tangible and identifiable intangible assets. It can be a place to hide overpayments or useless projects. When assessing a company, be wary of significant or increasing goodwill. Investigate its source and question whether it reflects real value or is a cover for imprudent acquisitions.

2. **Off-Balance Sheet Financing**

   Another technique companies use to improve their financial appearance is off-balance sheet financing. This involves moving liabilities to a separate entity or classifying them in a way that they don't appear as debt. Scrutinize the notes to the financial statements.

3. **Revenue Recognition**

   Revenue recognition manipulation is another common accounting trick. Companies might record revenue prematurely or for non-existent sales. If revenue is increasing, but cash flow is not, it could be a sign of aggressive revenue recognition.

4. Changes in Auditors

Frequent changes in auditors can be a red flag. While there could be legitimate reasons for changing auditors, it can also indicate that the company is trying to prevent the auditors from getting too familiar with their accounts or that auditors have found issues they're uncomfortable with.

5. Complex Corporate Structures

Companies with an unusually complex corporate structure can sometimes be a cause for concern. Multiple layers of subsidiaries or a convoluted network of inter-company transactions can be used to hide poor performance or shady dealings.

6. Excessive Executive Compensation

While high executive pay doesn't necessarily indicate fraud, it's worth scrutinizing if the executive compensation is vastly disproportionate to the company's size, profitability and performance. This could indicate that the company's governance isn't robust enough to prevent excessive pay packages.

7. Inconsistent Inventory Levels

If a company's inventory levels are consistently high relative to its sales, it could indicate that it's overvaluing its inventory or failing to write off obsolete items. This could artificially inflate the company's assets and earnings.

8. Disproportionate Growth in Accounts Receivable

A significant increase in accounts receivable relative to sales can be a sign that the company is recognizing revenue prematurely or for sales that may not be collectable.

Remember, each of these signs is not proof of wrongdoing, but they should prompt further investigation. As an investor, your goal is to gather as much information as possible to make an informed decision. It's always better to be cautious than to be sorry. Recognizing these signs doesn't mean the company is a bad investment. Instead, it's a prompt to dig deeper. Ask questions, do additional research and don't hesitate to walk away if things don't add up.

This chapter and its contents should be your final wall of defence. After you've found a company that appears fundamentally sound, growing, and at a reasonable price, use these insights to perform a final check. As the saying goes, 'Try to find a reason to say no as fast as possible.' If you can't find a reason, you might have found yourself a worthy investment.

Ultimately, the goal here is not to inspire fear but to encourage thoroughness and prudence in your investment journey. Keep in mind that most companies are not out to defraud investors. However, being aware of these red flags will help you separate the wheat from the chaff and ensure your investment decisions are based on a complete picture.

↗ Investing in Emerging Markets

While it's not accurate or fair to categorize all companies from Asia or emerging markets as risky or prone to fraudulent accounting practices, there are indeed unique risks associated with investing in these regions that investors should be aware of.

↗ Regulatory Environment

In some emerging markets, the regulatory environment might not be as robust or well-enforced as in developed countries. This could potentially make it easier for companies to engage in unethical or fraudulent behaviour without being detected.

↗ Transparency and Disclosure Standards

Companies in these regions may not have the same transparency and disclosure standards as their counterparts in more developed markets. This can make it more challenging for investors to get a clear and accurate picture of a company's financial health.

↗ Cultural and Language Barriers

Investing in foreign companies can also present challenges due to language barriers and differences in business culture. For example, the way business transactions are recorded or financial statements are prepared can differ significantly from what investors are used to in their home country.

That being said, investing in emerging markets can also offer significant opportunities for growth. As these economies grow and develop, companies in these regions can provide attractive investment opportunities.

Here are some recommendations for investors considering investing in these markets:

1. **Do your homework.**

It's important to do thorough due diligence before investing in any company, but this is especially true for companies in emerging markets. Ensure you understand the company's business model, financial health and the political and economic context in which it operates.

2. **Diversify.**

Spreading your investments across different countries and sectors can help mitigate the risks associated with investing in emerging markets.

3. **Seek professional advice.**

If you're unfamiliar with a particular market or region, it can be wise to seek advice from professionals who have expertise in that area. They can provide insights into the local business environment and potential red flags to watch out for.

4. **Use caution with individual stocks.**

If you're new to investing in emerging markets, it might be safer to start with mutual funds or ETFs that invest in a diversified portfolio of companies in these markets rather than investing in individual stocks.

Remember, every investment carries some level of risk, and it's important to understand and be comfortable with the risks you're taking before investing.

Moat and Investing

A 'moat' is a term popularized by renowned investor Warren Buffett to describe a company's sustainable competitive advantage that protects it from competition in the marketplace.

Just as a medieval castle's moat would protect it from invaders, a company's 'moat' serves to protect its market share and profits.

There are several types of economic moats that a company may possess.

Brand Moat

A strong, well-recognized brand can serve as a moat. Consumers trust these brands and are willing to pay a premium for their products or services, often making it difficult for new competitors to enter the market. Examples include companies like Apple or Coca-Cola.

Cost Moat

If a company can produce goods or services at a lower cost than its competitors, it has a cost moat. This allows the company to either undercut competitors in price or earn a higher profit margin. Companies like Walmart or Amazon, with their efficient supply chains and economies of scale, are examples.

Patent/Intellectual Property Moat

A company that owns valuable patents or intellectual property can prevent other companies from using its technology or inventions. This can provide a considerable advantage, especially in industries like pharmaceuticals or technology.

Switching Cost Moat

If it would be costly or inconvenient for customers to switch to a competitor's product or service, a company has a switching cost moat. This can occur in industries such as software or services. An example is Adobe's creative software suite.

Network Effect Moat

A company can have a network effect moat if its products or services become more valuable as more people use them.

Social media companies like Facebook and transaction companies like Visa are good examples.

These moats can protect a company's profits and market share, making it an attractive investment. However, investors should be aware that moats can erode over time due to factors like technological changes, regulatory changes, or shifts in consumer behaviour. Therefore, it's important to not just identify a company's moat but also to assess its sustainability over time. When building a fortress in the investment landscape, it's crucial to surround your financial kingdom with moats—competitive advantages that companies wield to ward off the competition. Let's explore the five types of moats that can make or break your investment decisions:

Intangible assets: These are the royal crests of the business world—brands, patents, and copyrights that command loyalty and price premiums. Take Coca-Cola, for example, a wide moat behemoth, whose secret recipe and global brand recognition are the envy of many kingdoms. On the other hand, Dr Pepper Snapple holds a respectable territory but lacks the vast dominion of Coca-Cola, signifying a narrower moat. United Airlines, despite its size, finds itself in the open fields without a significant moat, where its name doesn't command additional pricing power or fierce loyalty.

Switching costs: These are the drawbridges of a castle—once raised, it's costly and complex for the inhabitants (customers) to leave. Oracle has built a high wall, with its deeply entrenched databases forming an extensive moat. A business kingdom relying on Oracle would need to spend significant treasure and time to switch allegiance. Salesforce, while also fortified, has a narrower moat, as its subjects find switching a bit easier due to lower costs. Macy's, resembling a marketplace more than a fortress, faces the challenge of having virtually no moat, with customers free to come and go as they please.

Network effect: Picture a grand feast where each new guest adds to the revelry. The CME Group thrives on this effect, its clearinghouse functions becoming ever more potent as more traders join the banquet. NYSE Euronext, while also benefiting from the network effect, hosts a less exuberant feast, with fierce rivals vying for guests. ADM, on the other hand, sits alone at the table, with no significant network effect to speak of.

Cost advantage: Think of this as the kingdom's granary. UPS, with its ground delivery network, has a granary that never empties, allowing it to feed its subjects at a lower cost than its neighbours. FedEx, too, has a stocked granary but not as bountiful as UPS, showing a narrower moat. Alcoa's stores, conversely, face the threat of being overfilled, diminishing its cost advantage and eroding its moat.

Efficient scale: This moat is akin to a kingdom's control over a rare resource. Kinder Morgan reigns over its pipelines, its scale allowing it to monopolize the trade routes for energy. Southern Company, while holding significant territories, does not command the same level of control, hence a narrower moat. Paris Aeroport, without exclusive control over its skies and gates, confronts a world with no moat, leaving it vulnerable to the tides of competition.

In the game of thrones that is the business world, these moats are not just strategic; they are the bedrock of empires. As an investor, aligning your treasure with companies that boast such moats could mean the difference between a flourishing dominion and a forgotten fiefdom. Choose wisely, and may your investments be ever fortified.

5 Types Of MOATS

BY BRIAN FEROLDI

MOAT TYPE	INTANGIBLE ASSETS	SWITCHING COST	NETWORK EFFECT	COST ADVANTAGE	EFFICIENT SCALE
WIDE MOAT	Coca-Cola — It's sugar water, but consumers pay a premium for the brand name.	Oracle — Switching from Oracle's databases could cause massive disruptions.	CME Group — Its clearinghouse function keeps volume captive.	UPS — Ground delivery network have low marginal costs.	Kinder Morgan — Competitors have no incentive to enter.
NARROW MOAT	Dr Pepper Snapple — Good brands, but a lack of scale hurts returns.	Salesforce — A popular product, but switching costs are low for users.	NYSE Euronext — Equity volume is interchangeable and competitors have been aggressive.	FedEx — The high fixed-cost air segment is a large portion of revenue.	Southern Company — Regulators restrain returns.
NO MOAT	United Airlines — Name recognition doesn't result in pricing power.	Macy's — Consumers easily pick among many retailers.	ADM — Commoditized inputs and outputs prevent economic profits despite network.	Alcoa — Low-cost resources can't offset industry oversupply.	Paris — Geographic monopoly, but regulation prevents economic profit generation.

Source: Brian Feroldi & Morningstar

Source: Brian Feroldi & Morningstar

↗ Structure of a 10-K

The beautiful thing about a 10-K is that they all have the same structure. This means that the more 10-Ks you read, the faster and the better you'll get at it.

155

The structure of a 10-K looks like this:

1. **Business:** An overview of the company's main operations including its products and services. This section shows you how the company makes money so it's a good place to start. It's very important to **always invest within your circle of competence.** If you don't understand the business model, you can skip the company right away. **The business segment can usually be found at the beginning of the 10-K.**

2. **Risk factors**: Shows the major risks of the company. The risks are typically listed in order of importance. **Going through this section is very important.** As Benjamin Graham once said, 'The essence of investment management is the management of risks, not the management of returns.' When a company has a lot of goodwill on its balance sheet, generates a significant percentage of its revenue from a few clients, has low margins, or is active in a highly competitive market, it increases the risk for you as an investor.

3. **Financial statements**: Specific financial information about the business. As an investor, you want to buy **financially healthy companies with high margins and plenty of reinvestment opportunities**. That's why the financial statements are **one of the most important sections of a 10-K.** There are 3 Financial Statements in a 10-K:

    ○ **Balance sheet:** Gives you an overview of a company's main assets and liabilities. You want to invest in companies which don't have too much debt.

    ○ **Income statement:** Shows the company's revenues and expenses over a certain period. You want to invest in profitable companies which can grow their revenue organically at an attractive rate.

- **Cash flow statement:** Gives an overview of how much cash goes in and out of a company over a certain period. You want to invest in companies that are cash-flow-positive

4. **Management discussions and analysis (MD&A)**: Management's view on the business results of the past fiscal year. **It's always important to look at the qualitative factors behind the numbers.** That's why it's important that management can tell its story in its own words. Is the increasing revenue structural? Or is it because of a one-off event? **You want to invest in companies with an integer management with skin in the game.** Management should always give you a reliable view of the performance of the company. **Avoid companies that do not give an honest representation of their results.**

↗ Conclusion

- If you read the 10-K of a company you'll learn a lot and create a BIG advantage over other investors.

- A 10-K is an official document that is published every year.

- The 10-K can usually be found under the Investor Relations section of a company's website.

For a better understanding, and as an illustration, we will use Apple's latest annual report. An Annual Report consists of 4 parts. We will focus on the most important parts: 1. Business 2. Risk Factors 3. MD&A 4. Financial Statements (+Notes)

```
Apple Inc.
Form 10-K
For the Fiscal Year Ended September 24, 2022
TABLE OF CONTENTS
                                                                                Page
1)             Part I
   Item 1.    Business                                                            1
2) Item 1A.   Risk Factors                                                        5
   Item 1B.   Unresolved Staff Comments                                          17
   Item 2.    Properties                                                         17
   Item 3.    Legal Proceedings                                                  17
   Item 4.    Mine Safety Disclosures                                            17
              Part II
   Item 5.    Market for Registrant's Common Equity, Related Stockholder 
              Matters and Issuer Purchases of Equity Securities                  18
   Item 6.    [Reserved]                                                         19
3) Item 7.    Management's Discussion and Analysis of Financial 
              Condition and Results of Operations                                20
   Item 7A.   Quantitative and Qualitative Disclosures About Market Risk         26
4) Item 8.    Financial Statements and Supplementary Data                        28
   Item 9.    Changes in and Disagreements with Accountants 
              on Accounting and Financial Disclosure                             53
   Item 9A.   Controls and Procedures                                            53
   Item 9B.   Other Information                                                  54
   Item 9C.   Disclosure Regarding Foreign Jurisdictions that Prevent Inspections 54
              Part III
   Item 10.   Directors, Executive Officers and Corporate Governance             54
   Item 11.   Executive Compensation                                             54
   Item 12.   Security Ownership of Certain Beneficial Owners 
              and Management and Related Stockholder Matters                     54
   Item 13.   Certain Relationships and Related Transactions, 
              and Director Independence                                          54
   Item 14.   Principal Accountant Fees and Services                             54
              Part IV
   Item 15.   Exhibit and Financial Statement Schedules                          55
   Item 16.   Form 10-K Summary                                                  57
```

1. Business: The business section explains in simple terms what the firm offers and how it operates. This should always be the first thing you read. If you're not interested in the business or don't understand it, you're already done. Apple discusses the following topics:

2. Risk factors: This section is critical to your analysis. It discusses all the important risks the business faces. It's a great place to start with your assessment of the risks that investment could add to your portfolio. These are the topics discussed:

Item 1A. Risk Factors

Macroeconomic and Industry Risks

The Company's operations and performance depend significantly on global and regional economic conditions and adverse economic conditions can materially adversely affect the Company's business, results of operations and financial condition.

The Company's business, results of operations, financial condition and stock price have been adversely affected and could in the future be materially adversely affected by the COVID-19 pandemic.

The Company's business can be impacted by political events, trade and other international disputes, war, terrorism, natural disasters, public health issues, industrial accidents and other business interruptions.

Global markets for the Company's products and services are highly competitive and subject to rapid technological change, and the Company may be unable to compete effectively in these markets.

Business Risks

To remain competitive and stimulate customer demand, the Company must successfully manage frequent introductions and transitions of products and services.

The Company depends on component and product manufacturing and logistical services provided by outsourcing partners, many of which are located outside of the U.S.

Future operating results depend upon the Company's ability to obtain components in sufficient quantities on commercially reasonable terms.

The Company's products and services may be affected from time to time by design and manufacturing defects that could materially adversely affect the Company's business and result in harm to the Company's reputation.

The Company is exposed to the risk of write-downs on the value of its inventory and other assets, in addition to purchase commitment cancellation risk.

The Company relies on access to third-party intellectual property, which may not be available to the Company on commercially reasonable terms or at all.

Legal and Regulatory Compliance Risks

The Company's business, results of operations and financial condition could be adversely impacted by unfavorable results of legal proceedings or government investigations.

The Company is subject to complex and changing laws and regulations worldwide, which exposes the Company to potential liabilities, increased costs and other adverse effects on the Company's business.

Expectations relating to environmental, social and governance considerations expose the Company to potential liabilities, increased costs, reputational harm, and other adverse effects on the Company's business.

Financial Risks

The Company expects its quarterly net sales and results of operations to fluctuate.

The Company's financial performance is subject to risks associated with changes in the value of the U.S. dollar relative to local currencies.

General Risks

The price of the Company's stock is subject to volatility.

*These are short excerpts of the discussed contents

3. **MD&A** This section is, in some ways, the most interesting one. The management discusses the latest financials. They talk about margins, and external/internal factors on profitability and break down financials by product or region. It makes sense to compare this section to previous 10-Ks.

Item 7. Management's Discussion and Analysis of Financial Condition and Results of Operations

First Quarter 2022:
- Updated MacBook Pro 14" and MacBook Pro 16", powered by the Apple M1 Pro or M1 Max chip; and
- Third generation of AirPods.

Second Quarter 2022:
- Updated iPhone SE with 5G technology;
- All-new Mac Studio, powered by the Apple M1 Max or M1 Ultra chip;
- All-new Studio Display™; and
- Updated iPad Air with 5G technology, powered by the Apple M1 chip.

Third Quarter 2022:
- Updated MacBook Air and MacBook Pro 13", both powered by the Apple M2 chip;
- iOS 16, macOS Ventura, iPadOS 16 and watchOS 9, updates to the Company's operating systems; and
- Apple Pay Later, a buy now, pay later service.

Fourth Quarter 2022:
- iPhone 14, iPhone 14 Plus, iPhone 14 Pro and iPhone 14 Pro Max;
- Second generation of AirPods Pro; and
- Apple Watch Series 8, updated Apple Watch SE and all-new Apple Watch Ultra.

Products and Services Performance

The following table shows net sales by category for 2022, 2021 and 2020 (dollars in millions):

Net sales by category	2022	Change	2021	Change	2020
iPhone [1]	$ 205,489	7 %	$ 191,973	39 %	$ 137,781
Mac [1]	40,177	14 %	35,190	23 %	28,622
iPad [1]	29,292	(8)%	31,862	34 %	23,724
Wearables, Home and Accessories [1][2]	41,241	7 %	38,367	25 %	30,620
Services [1]	78,129	14 %	68,425	27 %	53,768
Total net sales	$ 394,328	8 %	$ 365,817	33 %	$ 274,515

Segment Operating Performance

Net sales by reportable segment	2022	Change	2021	Change	2020
Americas	$ 169,658	11 %	$ 153,306	23 %	$ 124,556
Europe	95,118	7 %	89,307	30 %	68,640
Greater China	74,200	9 %	68,366	70 %	40,308
Japan	25,977	(9)%	28,482	33 %	21,418
Rest of Asia Pacific	29,375	11 %	26,356	35 %	19,593
Total net sales	$ 394,328	8 %	$ 365,817	33 %	$ 274,515

Gross Margin

Products and Services gross margin and gross margin percentage for 2022, 2021 and 2020 were as follows (dollars in millions):

	2022	2021	2020
Gross margin:			
Products	$ 114,728	$ 105,126	$ 69,461
Services	56,054	47,710	35,495
Total gross margin	$ 170,782	$ 152,836	$ 104,956
Gross margin percentage:			
Products	36.3 %	35.3 %	31.5 %
Services	71.7 %	69.7 %	66.0 %
Total gross margin percentage	43.3 %	41.8 %	38.2 %

4. **Financial statements (+Notes)** I won't discuss the financial statements here. Here we'll focus on the notes. They are a great resource for extra information. Reading them will answer most of your remaining questions regarding the statements. They discuss accounting policies, financial instruments, accounts receivable, leases etc. Generally, they help you to dig deeper and understand the details of the financials. This is a quick way to get value from an annual report but is not the most thorough way.

As we close this chapter, consider the 10-K analysis of your treasure map; it points to where you should concentrate your energies. Your goal? To become an investment sleuth, swiftly uncovering clues that tell you whether to walk away from a stock. By mastering the art of a quick 'no', you free yourself to scour the market landscape for those hidden gems. Time is gold in the world of investing, and the faster you sift through the duds, the sooner you'll strike investment gold.

As an investor, it's essential to navigate the Annual Report/10-K of a company, documents that can sometimes feel like daunting epics with their hundreds of pages. The good news? You can now harness the power of AI to distil this tome into a digestible summary. However, the AI is only as good as the instructions you provide. In the next chapter, we'll explore strategies for efficiently dissecting a 10-K, pinpointing the critical information you need. We'll walk you through an example of how to focus your AI assistant on uncovering the insights that matter most, ensuring you're equipped to make informed investment decisions.

KEY TAKEAWAYS

- Corporate governance is crucial for companies to function in an accountable, fair and transparent manner, ensuring the interests of various stakeholders are considered.

- Good corporate governance builds trust and confidence among stakeholders, provides clear communication and promotes financial viability in the long run.

- Investors should assess a company's governance structure, board independence, risk management practices and financial disclosures to make informed investment decisions.

- Different regions have varied corporate governance models, each with its strengths and weaknesses, and companies should adopt an approach that suits their goals and values.

- Corporate scandals have led to increased regulatory changes, emphasizing the importance of ethical behaviour and transparency, with investors playing a crucial role in promoting good governance practices.

- Investors should be vigilant about recognizing signs of corporate fraud, conducting thorough research and asking questions before making investment decisions.

CHAPTER 7

TWO IMPORTANT APPROACHES TO INVESTING – GROWTH AND VALUE INVESTING

"It's tough to make predictions, especially about the future."

– Yogi Berra

Two Important Approaches to Investing – Growth and Value

Have you ever wondered how successful investors make decisions in the ever-changing market landscape? Do you find yourself torn between the allure of high-growth potential and the safety of undervalued stock opportunities? Well, I know you have many such questions, and this chapter aims to provide you with all the answers related to investing approaches. They will enable you to pick stocks that have the potential to grow over time.

In the vast world of investing, where countless strategies and approaches exist, two distinct and influential methodologies stand out: growth investing and value investing. These approaches have shaped the investment landscape and proven to be crucial for investors seeking to navigate the complexities of the market. Understanding these approaches is essential for anyone seeking to build a robust investment portfolio and make informed decisions.

Growth investing is characterized by focusing on companies expected to experience above-average growth rates in terms of their revenues, earnings or other key performance indicators. Investors employing a growth strategy seek out firms with the potential to expand rapidly due to factors such as innovative products, new market opportunities or disruptive technologies. The goal is to invest in companies that can generate substantial value over time by capitalizing on their growth potential.

Value investing, on the other hand, revolves around identifying stocks that appear to be trading below their intrinsic or book value. This strategy is rooted in the belief that the market sometimes undervalues companies for various reasons, such as temporary setbacks, market sentiment or overlooked opportunities. Value investors aim to capitalize on these instances of perceived undervaluation, expecting the market to eventually recognize the company's true worth, leading to price appreciation.

While both growth and value strategies have their merits, they also come with inherent risks that investors need to be aware of. Value investing, for instance, can lead to the phenomenon known as a 'value trap'. A value trap occurs when a stock's low valuation is justified due to fundamental issues within the company. These issues might include declining business performance, unfavourable industry trends or poor management decisions. While the stock may seem to be attractively priced, it can be a trap if the company's underlying problems prevent it from recovering or growing in the future. Investors who fall into value traps may find themselves holding onto a declining investment for an extended period, eroding their capital.

Growth investing, on the other hand, can expose investors to the risk of speculative behaviour. When investors focus solely on a company's growth potential without adequately considering its current valuation, they may end up paying inflated prices for stocks that don't necessarily justify their high valuations. This speculative behaviour can lead to situations where the stock's price becomes detached from its fundamental value. If the market sentiment shifts or the growth story loses credibility, the stock price can plummet, resulting in significant losses for investors.

Can you envision a scenario where these two seemingly opposing strategies might intersect and complement each other? Warren Buffett, a prominent figure in the world of investing, has shared valuable insights on these two approaches. He famously stated, 'Only when the tide goes out do you discover who's been swimming naked.' This metaphor underscores the importance of a balanced approach. Companies can hide their weaknesses during favourable market conditions, but market downturns expose these vulnerabilities. This underscores the need for considering both growth and value elements in an investment strategy.

Buffett's perspective challenges the notion of a strict divide between growth and value investing. He argues that growth and value are interconnected. His investment philosophy centres on buying quality companies at a fair price. According to Buffett, the concept of growth is an essential aspect of determining a company's value. This perspective suggests that investors don't have to choose one approach over the other but can instead blend the two, seeking out companies that offer both growth potential and reasonable valuation.

However, Buffett's approach also comes with a word of caution. While blending growth and value principles can be beneficial, investors must remain vigilant against falling into value traps. This requires conducting thorough due diligence, understanding a company's competitive positioning, industry trends and ability to execute growth strategies.

The distinction between growth and value investing is not always clear-cut. Both strategies have their strengths and weaknesses, and successful investing often involves a nuanced approach that considers both growth potential and fundamental valuation.

In this chapter, we will delve into the realms of growth and value investing, uncovering their defining characteristics, exploring how they can overlap, highlighting their differences, and providing tangible real-world stock examples to illustrate their practical applications. By understanding the intricacies of these strategies and heeding the insights of seasoned investors like Warren Buffett, individuals can navigate the complexities of the market with greater confidence and make informed decisions that align with their investment goals and risk tolerance. Remember that investment decisions should be based on thorough research, a clear understanding of the company's fundamentals, and a long-term perspective that considers both growth and value.

↗ Growth Investing

Growth investing focuses on identifying companies with the potential for significant future growth. Investors who follow this approach typically seek out companies that demonstrate strong revenue and earnings growth, often in emerging industries or with innovative products or services. The primary goal is to invest in companies that can deliver above-average returns over the long term.

Key Characteristics of Growth Investing

1. **Emphasis on future potential**

   Growth investors focus on a company's future growth prospects rather than its current value. They believe that by investing in companies with strong growth potential, they can benefit from the compounding effect over time. These companies are often at an early stage of development or have disruptive business models that can lead to substantial expansion in the future.

2. **Higher valuation**

   Growth stocks tend to have higher price-to-earnings (P/E) ratios as investors are willing to pay a premium for anticipated growth. Investors are optimistic about the company's prospects and are willing to accept a higher valuation in the hopes of significant future returns. This higher valuation reflects the market's expectation of future growth and can lead to volatility in the stock price.

3. **Reinvestment of earnings**

   Growth companies often reinvest their profits back into the business to fuel further expansion. They prioritize using their earnings to finance research and development, marketing, acquisitions, or other initiatives that can drive future growth. By reinvesting earnings, these companies aim to capture a larger market share, develop new products or services, and increase their competitive advantage.

🡵 Real Stock Example for Growth Investing

One compelling illustration of growth investing is Amazon.com Inc. (NASDAQ: AMZN). Since its IPO in 1997, Amazon's stock price has skyrocketed, growing from around $18 per share to over $3,000 per share as of the end of 2021 before it went for a stock split in the ratio of 20:1 in 2022. This remarkable growth is a testament to the company's ability to innovate and disrupt traditional industries. In addition, Amazon's revenue has surged from $147 million in 1997 to a staggering $524.897 billion in 2023, showcasing its phenomenal growth trajectory. Furthermore, its market capitalization has surged from around $400 million at the time of its IPO to over $1.17 trillion, making it one of the most valuable companies in the world. These staggering figures highlight the immense growth potential and long-term success that growth investors seek when investing in companies with promising future prospects.

🡵 Integration of Contrarian and Value Investing

Contrarian investing is an investment strategy that involves making decisions that go against prevailing market sentiment and trends. In other words, contrarian investors actively seek out opportunities in assets or markets that are currently out of favour or undervalued by the majority of investors. The goal of contrarian investing is to take advantage of situations where assets are priced lower than their intrinsic value due to market overreactions, emotions or misconceptions.

Contrarian investing requires a strong understanding of market dynamics, a contrarian mindset, and the ability to differentiate between short-term market noise and genuine opportunities. It's important to note that contrarian investing can involve higher risks due to the potential for prolonged periods of undervaluation or unfavourable market conditions. As with any investment strategy, thorough research, analysis and risk management are essential for success in contrarian investing.

Peter Lynch, a legendary investor and former manager of the Magellan Fund, was known for his contrarian growth investing approach. Lynch believed that opportunities for exceptional growth often lie in out-of-favour companies or industries. One notable example is his investment in Dunkin' Donuts. In the 1980s, when investors were sceptical about the prospects of a doughnut chain, Lynch saw the growth potential and invested heavily. His contrarian move paid off, as Dunkin' Donuts became a phenomenal success, contributing to the remarkable performance of the Magellan Fund.

While contrarian and value investing have distinct approaches, they can be complementary when integrated effectively.

Undervalued opportunities: Contrarian investing identifies assets that are temporarily undervalued due to market sentiment. By combining this approach with value investing's emphasis on fundamental analysis, investors can identify assets that are not only sentiment-driven but also fundamentally sound.

Margin of safety: Both strategies prioritize a margin of safety, albeit in different ways. Contrarian investing's margin of safety comes from the expectation of sentiment-driven price reversals, while value investing's margin of safety is derived from the discrepancy between intrinsic value and market price. By combining these approaches, investors can potentially achieve a more robust margin of safety.

Long-term potential: Both strategies require a long-term perspective. Contrarian investors need patience for sentiment to shift, while value investors await the realization of a company's true worth. The integration of these strategies reinforces the need for a patient, long-term approach.

Risk management: Contrarian investors may find comfort in value investing's rigorous assessment of fundamental strengths. Value investing can provide a solid foundation for contrarian investment decisions, reducing the risk of investing solely based on sentiment.

Balanced diversification: Integrating both strategies can lead to a balanced portfolio with diversified assets that offer the potential for both sentiment-driven and fundamental-driven gains.

Key Characteristics of Value Investing

Emphasis on intrinsic value

Value investors analyze a company's fundamentals, such as its balance sheet, earnings, cash flow and other metrics, to determine its true worth. They seek to understand the underlying value of a company and invest when the market price is significantly below that intrinsic value. This approach aims to capitalize on market inefficiencies and take advantage of temporary mispricing. We will discuss more about it when we talk about the valuation of stocks and its related concepts like intrinsic value, discounted cash flow (DCF), and reverse DCF later in this chapter.

Warren Buffett's quote, 'Price is what you pay, and value is what you get,' captures the essence of investing, especially in the context of the stock market. The graph below illustrates the journey of a stock's price over time.

WHAT IS VALUE INVESTING?

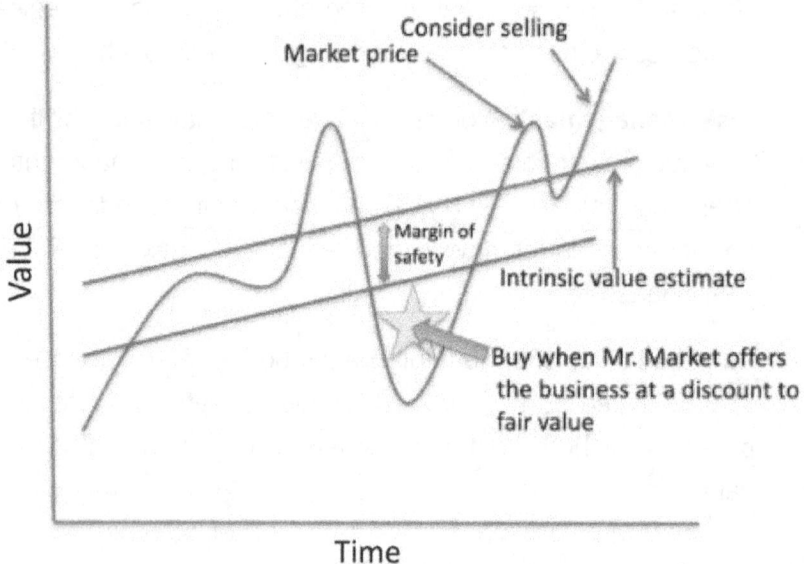

Source: https://www.nasdaq.com/articles/how-be-successful-value-investor-2019-04-12

The market price line resembles a roller coaster, with sharp fluctuations that can evoke excitement and anxiety. Contrastingly, the intrinsic value line paints a consistent upward trajectory, reflecting stability. At first glance, the average change in market price might seem implausible. How could a company's value change so drastically in just a year?

The answer lies in the intricacies of the market. Price swings reflect dynamic forces like economic conditions, investor sentiment and trends. The volatility can lead to sudden price spikes or drops, often unrelated to the company's actual worth.

In contrast, the intrinsic value line's steady rise is anchored in the company's fundamentals – earnings, growth potential and competitive position. These aspects don't shift overnight. The seemingly extreme average market price change arises from short-term price movements, often influenced by sentiment rather than actual value.

In this scenario, the divergence between price and value highlights the market's complexity. It reinforces the need for a long-term perspective, emphasizing intrinsic value over short-term price fluctuations. While the market may be turbulent, a wise investor recognizes that genuine value persists, even amid price volatility.

Lower valuation
Value stocks tend to have lower price-to-earnings (P/E) ratios and other valuation metrics, making them appear cheaper relative to their earnings or assets. In addition, value investors look for stocks trading at a discount to their intrinsic value, providing a margin of safety. This discount may arise due to factors such as negative market sentiment, industry-specific challenges, or temporary setbacks faced by the company.

Margin of safety
Value investors seek a margin of safety by purchasing stocks below their intrinsic value to protect against potential downside risks. They believe buying stocks at a significant discount can minimize losses if the market recognizes the company's true value. This approach provides a buffer against unexpected events or adverse market conditions.

Real stock example for value investing

International Business Machines Corporation (IBM) (NYSE: IBM) is a prominent example of value investing. In 2008, IBM faced challenges due to the prevailing financial crisis. During this period, the stock price declined significantly, trading around $66.

However, value investors saw the potential in the company's strong fundamentals, extensive intellectual property and long-standing reputation in the industry, which resulted in a positive turnaround for the company. In early 2013, IBM's stock price was trading at around $200 per share.

Over time, IBM embarked on a strategic transformation, focusing on emerging technologies such as cloud computing, artificial intelligence and data analytics. As a result, the stock price gradually recovered as the company progressed in its turnaround efforts.

By the end of 2021, IBM's stock price had reached approximately $130 per share, representing a modest but noteworthy recovery. Additionally, value investors were rewarded with consistent dividend payments. For instance, in 2013, IBM's annual dividend was $3.80 per share, and by 2021, it had increased to $6.52 per share, demonstrating the company's commitment to providing value to shareholders.

This example of IBM highlights the potential of value investing by identifying undervalued companies with strong fundamentals that have the potential to rebound and generate long-term value. Value investors who recognized IBM's potential during its challenging period and were patient in their investment strategy were rewarded with both capital appreciation and increasing dividend payments as the company executed its turnaround plan.

Differences Between Growth and Value Investing

Despite some overlap, there are significant differences between growth and value investing. The key distinctions include:

Investment philosophy

Growth investing and value investing have distinct investment philosophies:

Growth investing focuses on future growth potential and the ability to generate substantial returns over time. As a result, investors in growth stocks are often optimistic about the company's prospects and are willing to pay a higher valuation to participate in the anticipated growth.

Value investing emphasizes identifying undervalued stocks and capitalizing on market inefficiencies. Value investors aim to buy stocks below their intrinsic value, considering them bargains and anticipating that the market will eventually recognize their true worth.

Valuation metrics

Growth investing and value investing employ different valuation metrics to evaluate stocks:

Growth investing relies on metrics such as price-to-earnings growth (PEG) ratio, sales growth rate, and forward-looking indicators. These metrics reflect the company's growth potential and its ability to deliver future earnings expansion.

Value investing focuses on valuation ratios like price-to-earnings (P/E), price-to-book (P/B), and dividend yield. In addition, value investors assess the company's financial health, asset values, and income generation capabilities to determine whether the stock is undervalued.

Risk and volatility

Growth and value stocks differ in terms of risk and volatility.

Growth stocks often exhibit higher volatility and may be subject to greater market risk due to their higher valuations and growth expectations. The market's perception of a growth stock's potential can lead to price swings, both positive and negative, as investors reassess their growth projections.

Value stocks, while potentially less volatile, can carry their own risks if the underlying company's fundamentals deteriorate further. Value investors seek to mitigate risk by identifying companies with strong financials and a margin of safety. However, if the company fails to recover or experiences further setbacks, the investment may not realize its full potential.

↗ **Overlap Between Growth and Value Investing**

Although growth and value investing are distinct approaches, there can be areas of overlap. In certain situations, a stock may simultaneously possess growth and value characteristics. For instance:

A growth stock may experience a temporary setback, causing its price to decline and making it attractive to value investors. These value investors may identify the stock's underlying growth potential and consider it an opportunity to invest at a discounted price.

A value stock may demonstrate growth potential due to industry tailwinds, strategic initiatives or new product launches, making it appealing to growth investors. If a value stock is positioned to capitalize on emerging trends or has a catalyst that can drive future growth, growth investors may find it attractive despite its current undervaluation.

The overlap between growth and value investing highlights the dynamic nature of the stock market and the potential for different investment strategies to converge in certain situations. As a result, investors can benefit from understanding the interplay between growth and value factors when evaluating investment opportunities.

⏷ The Wisdom of Warren Buffett: 'Forget About Value vs. Growth Investing.'

If there's anyone whose investing wisdom we should listen to, it's Warren Buffett. With a net worth of over $100 billion as of 2023, Buffett is often regarded as one of the most successful investors of all time. One of his many insightful views on investing strategy relates to the often-contentious dichotomy of value and growth investing. According to a **Motley Fool report**, Buffett thinks this differentiation is unnecessary, and here's why.

Warren Buffett has a history of redefining commonly held investing principles, and this case is no different. According to him, the division between value and growth investing is artificial and pointless. He famously stated, 'Growth and value investing are joined at the hip.' This means that, to Buffett, growth is simply a component of value.

As we've said, value investors look for stocks that they believe are undervalued by the market. The idea is to buy these stocks at a discount and make a profit when the market corrects itself. On the other hand, growth investors focus on stocks that display above-average growth, regardless of their current valuation. In Buffett's view, this distinction doesn't exist. He believes that all investing is value investing. What's more, he argues that growth is always a factor in calculating value. In other words, a company's potential for growth is one of the variables that determine its intrinsic value.

Buffett's philosophy revolves around buying great businesses at good prices and holding onto them for a long time. He views growth as a component of a company's overall value, suggesting that investors should be seeking companies that have strong growth potential and are also undervalued by the market.

It's crucial to note that Buffett doesn't suggest that growth should be the only variable to consider when calculating value. It's just one of many aspects. Other factors to consider include the company's management, financial health, competitive advantage, and market conditions. However, the main takeaway is that growth should not be disregarded when looking for value investments.

So, the next time you find yourself caught in the value vs. growth debate, remember the words of Warren Buffett. Don't make investing more complicated than it needs to be. Focus on the fundamentals of the company, consider its growth prospects as a part of its value, and always aim to buy at a price that offers a margin of safety.

↗ Valuation of Stocks – Navigating the Complexities of Worth and Value

A common misconception in investing is that complex

formulas are necessary for determining a company's fair value. However, as many investment professionals would attest, pursuing precision to two decimal places is a misguided approach. This is because calculating a company's intrinsic value requires a plethora of assumptions. John Maynard Keynes once said, 'It is better to be roughly right than precisely wrong,' emphasizing the importance of reasonable estimates over false precision.

Furthermore, Charlie Munger, Warren Buffett's business partner and vice-chairman of Berkshire Hathaway, has been known to say, 'Some of the worst business decisions I've seen came with detailed analysis. The higher math was false precision. They do that in business schools because they've got to do something.' Munger's perspective underscores the concept that investing isn't about complex formulas or detailed analysis but rather about making reasonable estimations.

So, how can we determine whether a stock is cheap or expensive without resorting to complicated calculations? The answer lies in understanding a company's fair value.

⤻ Intrinsic Value of a Company and Discounted Cash Flow (DCF)

A company's intrinsic value represents the present value of all cash it is likely to generate over its remaining lifetime. Imagine you have a golden goose named ABC Inc., and this golden goose will continue to lay golden eggs for the next ten years before it retires. It is anticipated that ABC Inc. will produce $15 worth of golden eggs per year. Thus, over ten years, ABC Inc. will generate $150 worth of golden eggs. This total of $150 is the intrinsic value of the golden goose, or, as in the case of a business, the company.

However, due to inflation, the value of money decreases over time. This is why we need to calculate the discounted value of future cash flow, not just the face value. The discounted value considers that money you receive in the future will not have the same buying power as today. The graph below reveals the decreasing value of money over time at different inflation ratios.

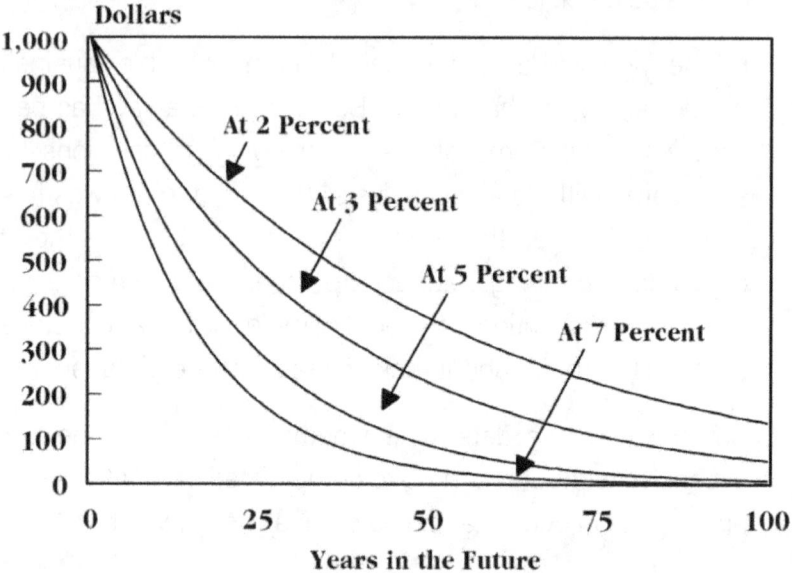

Source: https://en.wikipedia.org/wiki/Time_value_of_money#/media/File:Economics_of_climate_change_chapter3_discounting_curves.png

If we aim to make an annual return of 10% from our investment (this is the discount rate), we can calculate the intrinsic value (discounted future cash flows) of ABC Inc. After doing this calculation, you find that the intrinsic value is around $92.2. So, if you can acquire ABC Inc. for $92.2 or less, you will achieve a return of at least 10% per year.

↗ Implied Growth Rate

Remember, the intrinsic value we calculate is essentially the current price that we believe is fair, based on our expectation of future cash flows and our desired return rate. But what does this mean for our expected return if we buy at the current market price, not our calculated intrinsic price? This is where the concept of implied growth rate becomes important. The implied growth rate is the rate of growth that the current market price assumes.

Reverse Discounted Cash Flow (DCF)

The examples we used above are overly simplified because, in real life, no company can grow its Free Cash Flow (FCF) at the same rate forever. That's where Reverse DCF comes into play, and it's one of the best ways to value a company.

Reverse DCF helps you understand what growth rate the market has factored into the current stock price. If you think the company can grow faster than the market's implied growth rate, then the stock may be undervalued.

Munger advises that it's helpful to revert or backtrack when trying to solve a complex problem. In the context of investing, instead of trying to calculate a company's value, look at the stock price and decipher what it implies about the company's future. Thus, you can understand if the company's value is realistic and achievable based on current stock prices.

That's a broad overview of the key concepts, but there's a lot more depth to this topic! Here are a few more things to keep in mind when using this kind of analysis.

1. **Future predictability:** This method's validity hinges on your ability to accurately predict a company's future free cash flows. In practice, this is often difficult due to various uncertainties surrounding business and market

conditions. Companies in more stable industries might have more predictable cash flows, while those in rapidly changing industries might be more difficult to forecast.

2. **Other factors:** A company's future cash flows aren't the only things that matter. You should also consider other important factors such as the company's financial health, competitive position, quality of management, and so on. This kind of analysis should be part of a more comprehensive evaluation of a company.

3. **Discount rate:** The discount rate is a critical part of this calculation, and it's often subjective. Some investors use the risk-free rate (like the return on a government bond) plus a risk premium, while others might use their desired rate of return.

4. **Growth assumptions:** The assumption that the growth rate of FCF per share remains constant over 10 years may not be accurate, especially for industries or companies that are rapidly changing. In these cases, a stage-wise growth rate assumption might be more suitable.

5. **Limitations of DCF:** While DCF can be a powerful tool for investment valuation, it has limitations. For example, it's less useful for companies that don't have consistent, positive free cash flow. Plus, as mentioned above, its accuracy depends largely on the accuracy of your assumptions.

Lastly, remember that investing always carries risks, and it's important to thoroughly understand these concepts and risks before making any investment decisions. Always do your research or consult with a financial advisor if you're unsure. Now that you have a broad understanding of valuation, growth and intrinsic value, here are a few exercises for you which will enable you to test your investing skills.

- Select a publicly traded company and perform a simple Reverse DCF analysis to estimate the implied growth rate that the market is assuming for that company's future growth.

- Choose a well-known company and perform a basic DCF analysis to estimate its intrinsic value. Consider different scenarios for growth rates and discount rates to see how they impact the calculated value.

- Research a company that faced challenges in the past but managed to turn its fortunes around. Analyse how value investing principles could have been applied to identify its potential and the factors that contributed to its recovery.

Identify a stock that you believe is currently undervalued based on your analysis. Use the implied growth rate method to understand the market's growth assumptions and evaluate whether you agree with them.

Do you remember what our friend Yogi Berra said at the beginning of this chapter? 'It's tough to make predictions, especially about the future.' Reflecting on our discussion, you might wonder why we traversed this topic if it seems to circle back to where we began. The truth is, understanding growth and value investing, and the complexities of future predictions, is crucial, even if it feels like a paradox. Remember, the kind of growth that truly matters isn't the speculative growth of the future, which remains shrouded in uncertainty. **Rather, it's the growth traced in the past—a consistent and stable growth trajectory—that you should seek.**

As for the concepts of value investing and reverse cash flow, they might seem like they require a crystal ball to be truly effective. A company's future earnings are often speculative at best. Instead of getting lost in the complexities of forecasting, I encourage you to revisit Chapter 5. Ground your investment decisions in the tangible and the known. Understand where your money is going, focusing on historical performance as a more reliable guide than speculative future earnings.

In essence, while pondering the future can offer insights, anchoring your investment strategy in solid, historical data and a clear understanding of where your money currently stands will serve you best on your investing journey.

KEY TAKEAWAYS

- Growth and value investing are two important approaches to consider when building an investment portfolio.

- Growth investing can lead to speculative behaviour and detachment of stock prices from fundamental value. Value investing can lead to value traps, where stocks are cheap for valid reasons and may not recover. Both approaches require careful consideration to avoid potential pitfalls.

- Growth is a component of determining a company's value. Blending growth and value principles can lead to a balanced approach that considers both growth potential and reasonable valuation. Even Warren Buffett emphasizes that growth and value investing are interconnected.

- Valuing stocks involves calculating their intrinsic value, which is the present value of all future cash flows. This can be done using methods like discounted cash flow (DCF) analysis, Reverse DCF, and implied growth rate analysis.

- Protection in value investing: When investments in so-called 'value traps' face challenges, investors still have a safety net through the company's tangible assets, cash reserves and dividends. These elements provide a buffer, reducing potential losses.

- Risks of growth investing: Conversely, when investments in 'growth traps' falter, investors' fortunes hinge on external factors or 'the kindness of strangers'. Without tangible assets or dividends to fall back on, the risk is significantly higher, as future growth expectations may not materialize.

CHAPTER 8

DECODING THE COMPOUNDING POWER FOR CREATING WEALTH

"Successful investing is about having people agree with you… later."

– James Grant

Have you ever wondered how small actions can lead to significant outcomes over time? Think about saving a little money regularly – could that grow into substantial wealth? What if I tell you there is a financial phenomenon that could turn your modest investments into a potential goldmine? Imagine investments multiplying quietly in the background – does that sound too good to be true? Well, in the world of investing, there is a phenomenon that has the power to transform modest investments into significant wealth over time. It is known as the compounding effect.

This chapter aims to unravel the true significance of compounding in relation to investing, explore how investors can harness its power to create substantial wealth, provide real examples of stocks where the compounding effect has greatly benefited investors, and delve into other aspects and topics associated with this financial principle. By understanding and leveraging the compounding effect, readers will gain insights and strategies to make informed investment decisions that have the potential to yield impressive long-term returns.

↗ Understanding Compounding in Investing

To truly understand the concept of compounding, consider the game of snowballing. When a small snowball is rolled down a snow-covered hill, it starts picking up more snow, growing larger and rolling faster with each passing moment. In the beginning, the growth seems slow and almost unnoticeable. However, as it continues its journey down the hill, the rate of growth accelerates rapidly. The snowball, which was initially small and slow, transforms into a large, fast-moving entity.

Similarly, compounding is a process that involves generating earnings from both the initial investment and the accumulated returns over time. At first, the earnings might seem minimal, but as you reinvest those earnings, they start to generate returns. As time goes by, your investment, like the snowball, begins to grow faster and larger.

This snowballing effect allows investors to earn returns not just on their principal amount but also on the gains or dividends earned from previous periods. In other words, compounding involves reinvesting the earnings from investments to generate even greater returns in subsequent periods. This compounding growth can significantly amplify investment returns and was often described as the 'eighth wonder of the world' by legendary physicist Albert Einstein.

Much like the snowball, the power of compounding may not be apparent in the early stages. However, given enough time, the growth becomes significant and can lead to substantial wealth creation. This is why starting early and remaining patient are key factors when harnessing the power of compounding in investing.

To illustrate the power of compounding, let's consider an example. Suppose you invest $5,000 in a mutual fund that delivers an average annual return of 10%. Here's how your investment might grow over time if all returns are reinvested:

- After one year, your investment would grow to $5,500 ($5,000 + $5,000 * 10%).

- In the second year, you're not just earning interest on your initial $5,000 but also on the $500 gain from the first year. So, your investment would grow to $6,050 ($5,500 + $5,500 * 10%).

- In the third year, you earn interest on $6,050, making your investment worth $6,655 ($6,050 + $6,050 * 10%).

As you can see, with each passing year, your investment grows more significantly due to the interest earned on both the initial amount and the accumulated interest from previous years - that's compounding in action!

The Rule of 72
The Rule of 72 is a simple formula used to estimate how long it will take for an investment to double, given a fixed annual rate of return. You simply divide 72 by the annual rate of return.

For example, if you expect an 8% annual return, you will calculate 72 / 8 = 9 years. This means it would take roughly nine years for your investment to double at an 8% rate of return.

This rule provides a quick and easy way to understand the potential impact of compounding on investment over time. However, it's important to remember that it's an approximation, and real investment outcomes may be influenced by various factors such as market volatility, changes in interest rates, and investment fees.

The Power of Compounding in Wealth Creation
Compounding has the remarkable ability to accelerate wealth creation over long periods. The key to harnessing this power lies in starting early and allowing investments to grow over time. The longer the investment horizon, the greater the compounding effect. By reinvesting earnings, whether through dividends, interest, or capital gains, investors can benefit from the exponential growth potential that compounding offers. This means that the earlier an individual starts investing and the longer they stay invested, the greater the impact of compounding on their wealth.

Harnessing the Power of Dividends

Dividends play a vital role in the compounding process. When a company earns a profit, it can distribute a portion of these earnings to shareholders in the form of dividends. Investors can choose to take these dividends as cash, or they can opt to reinvest them back into the company by purchasing more shares. This process of reinvesting dividends is a key driver of compounding.

One common method of reinvesting dividends is through a Dividend Reinvestment Plan (DRIP). A DRIP is a program offered by many companies that allows investors to automatically reinvest their cash dividends into additional shares or fractional shares of the underlying stock on the dividend payment date. Instead of receiving quarterly dividend checks, participating shareholders will have their dividends used to purchase more shares of the company's stock.

To illustrate, let's say you own 100 shares of a company that pays a yearly dividend of $1 per share, and the current share price is $20. Over the year, you'd receive $100 in dividends. With a DRIP, instead of taking this $100 as cash, it would be used to buy five additional shares of the company (100/20 = 5). Now, instead of owning 100 shares, you own 105 shares. The next time dividends are paid, you'll receive dividends not just for your original 100 shares but for the additional five shares as well. As this process repeats over time, the number of shares you own – and the total dividends you receive – can grow significantly.

This automatic reinvestment of dividends facilitates the compounding effect and can lead to substantial growth in an investor's portfolio over time. It's one example of how the power of compounding can work to an investor's advantage.

Real Examples of Compounding in Stocks

The Coca-Cola Company (NYSE: KO)
Coca-Cola is a prime example of the compounding effect in action. The company has a long history of consistently increasing dividends for over six decades. Investors who held Coca-Cola shares and reinvested dividends over time witnessed remarkable growth. For instance, let's consider a hypothetical scenario. If an individual had invested $10,000 in Coca-Cola stock in 1980 and diligently reinvested all dividends received, his investment would have grown to over $1 million by 2021. This staggering growth demonstrates the power of compounding and its long-term wealth-creation potential.

Microsoft Corporation (NASDAQ: MSFT)
Microsoft is another exemplary case of the compounding effect. The company has experienced significant growth over the years and has consistently delivered value to its shareholders. For instance, let's imagine an individual had invested $10,000 in Microsoft stock in 1990 and reinvested all dividends received. By 2021, his investment would have grown to approximately $2.5 million. This substantial growth showcases how compounding can work its magic and generate significant wealth for patient and disciplined investors.

Apple Inc. (NASDAQ: AAPL)
Apple is a tech giant that has been at the forefront of innovation. In addition, it has demonstrated the power of compounding through its stock performance. For example, let's consider an individual who invested $10,000 in Apple stock in 2005 and reinvested all dividends received. By 2021, his investment would have grown to approximately $2 million.

This phenomenal growth illustrates the compounding effect and its wealth-building potential.

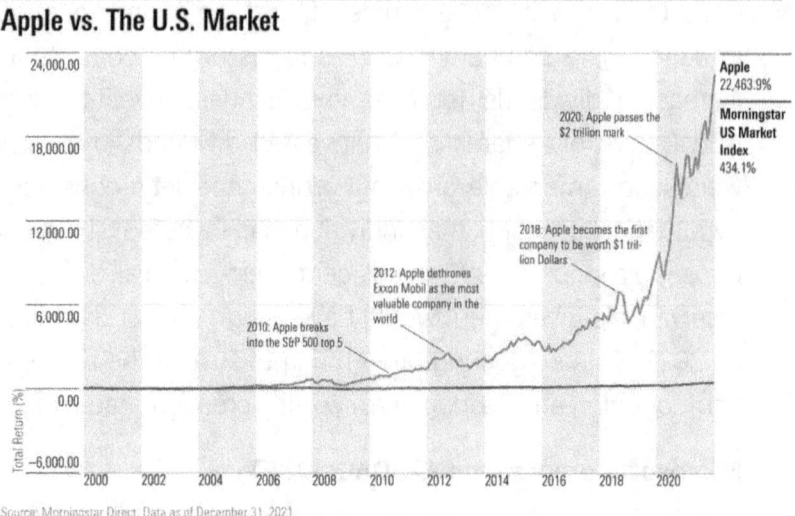

Source: https://www.morningstar.co.uk/uk/news/217520/apple-is-on-the-brink-of-becoming-a-%243-trillion-dollar-company.aspx

Visa Inc. (NYSE: V)

Visa, a leading global payments technology company, has been a rewarding investment for long-term shareholders. For example, suppose an individual invested $10,000 in Visa stock in 2008 and reinvested all dividends received. By 2021, his investment would have grown to over $100,000.

Blockbuster Inc.

On the other end of the spectrum, let's consider Blockbuster, a once-dominant video rental company. Suppose an individual had invested $10,000 in Blockbuster stock in 1994, the year the company was at its peak. The company experienced a steady decline with the advent of digital streaming platforms like Netflix, resulting in significant negative returns over the years. If the individual held onto the shares without selling, the investment would have been virtually worthless when the company declared bankruptcy in 2010.

In this case, the power of compounding did not work favourably due to the company's consistent negative returns. It serves as a reminder that while compounding can amplify gains, it can also accelerate losses if the investment continually declines in value. It emphasizes the importance of due diligence, diversification, and risk management in investing.

The examples of Coca-Cola, Microsoft, Apple, Visa, and Blockbuster illustrate the range of outcomes that can occur with investing. They highlight the power of compounding but also underscore the importance of investing in companies with solid fundamentals, strong business models, and good growth prospects. Compounding can generate significant wealth over time when paired with prudent investment decisions. However, investors should also be mindful of the potential risks, as investments can also decline in value.

Other Aspects and Topics Related to Compounding

Time Horizon and Impact of Rate of Return on Compounding

The time horizon is a critical factor in determining the compounding effect's magnitude. The longer the investment horizon, the greater the potential for compounding to work its magic. This emphasizes the importance of starting early and giving investments ample time to grow. Even small investments made early in life can accumulate substantial wealth through the power of compounding.

Let's illustrate this with a simple example:

Suppose you invest $10,000 in a mutual fund that delivers an average annual return of 5%. If you keep your money invested for 20 years, the compounding effect will grow your investment to approximately $26,533. However, if you extend the investment period to 30 years, the same investment grows to around $43,219. That's a significant increase solely due to the additional time the investment had to compound. This illustrates why starting early and staying invested for the long term is often encouraged in investment strategies.

The rate of return on investment is another crucial factor that influences the compounding effect. Higher rates of return lead to more substantial compounding benefits over time. Let's use the same investment example but change the rate of return:

If you invest $10,000 in a mutual fund with an average annual return of 5%, after 30 years, the investment grows to around $43,219. However, if the average annual return is 7%, the same investment over the same period grows to approximately $76,123.

A small difference in the rate of return can have a considerable impact on the final investment value due to compounding. However, it's essential to bear in mind that investments offering higher returns often come with higher risk. Therefore, it's crucial to align your investment choices with your risk tolerance, financial goals, and investment timeline.

Hence, both the length of time an investment is held and the rate of return play vital roles in harnessing the power of compounding. When these two factors work together, they can help transform modest investments into substantial wealth over time.

An excellent way to see the power of compounding in action is through a compounding calculator, investor.gov. This simple tool allows you to enter different variables—your initial investment, the expected rate of return, the number of years you plan to invest, and the frequency of compounding. With these inputs, the calculator can project how your investment might grow over time.

Imagine you invest an initial amount of $10,000 with an annual return of 8%, and you plan to stay invested for 20 years. You also decide to add $200 to your investment every month. Using these inputs in a compounding calculator, you can visualize the growth of your investment over the 20 years.

Moreover, you can experiment with different scenarios. What if you increase the amount you contribute every month? Or if you invest for a longer period? The compounding calculator allows you to explore these scenarios, underscoring the incredible power of compounding.

Risk and Return Trade-Off
While compounding offers significant benefits, it is vital to consider the risk-return trade-off inherent in investing. Investments that promise higher returns often come with a higher level of risk. Understanding this trade-off is crucial to making informed investment decisions.

Let's delve deeper into this concept. For instance, consider stocks and bonds. Stocks are typically seen as higher-risk investments. They can offer significant returns, especially over the long term, but they also come with a higher degree of volatility. This means the value of a stock investment can fluctuate widely, potentially leading to substantial gains or losses.

On the other hand, bonds are often viewed as lower-risk investments. They provide regular interest payments and return the principal amount at maturity. However, the overall returns from bonds are generally lower than those from stocks. While they offer more stability, they may not provide the level of return needed to achieve substantial compounding growth over time.

Then we have mutual funds, which are a mix of different types of investments (like stocks and bonds), providing diversification. While a mutual fund has the potential to provide good returns and compound growth, the level of risk and return would depend on its underlying investments.

Remember, it's not about avoiding risk but about understanding and managing it. An investor's risk tolerance, investment goals, and time horizon are key factors in determining the suitable level of risk.

Diversification, or spreading investments across a variety of different assets, and a well-defined investment strategy can help mitigate risk while capitalizing on compounding opportunities. For instance, an investor might choose to invest in a mix of stocks and bonds to balance potential returns with risk. So, as you seek to harness the power of compounding, remember the crucial role that the risk-return trade-off plays in the investing journey. A thoughtful approach to balancing risk and return can help you make the most of the compounding effect. We will discuss more about risk management in the next chapter when we talk about diversification.

Regular Contributions and Dollar-Cost Averaging

Regularly contributing to investments is a powerful strategy to enhance the compounding effect. By investing a fixed amount at regular intervals, investors can take advantage of market fluctuations and purchase more shares when prices are low. This approach, known as dollar-cost averaging, allows investors to build their investment base steadily and benefit from the compounding effect over time.

Let's understand this with an example. Consider two individuals, Jack and Jill, both of whom plan to invest in the stock market. They start with the same initial amount and expect the same average annual return, but they have different investment strategies.

Jack, believing in the power of lump sum investing, puts his entire savings of $12,000 into the stock market at the beginning of the year. Jill, on the other hand, decides to invest $1,000 at the start of every month, thereby investing the same total amount as Jack over the year. This approach is known as dollar-cost averaging.

Fast forward 20 years, assuming an annual return of 8%, Jack's investment has grown to approximately $55,200. However, Jill's investment, despite experiencing the ups and downs of the market, has grown to approximately $59,300.

Despite the market's volatility, Jill's regular investment approach allowed her to purchase more shares when prices were low, effectively reducing her average cost per share over time.

This example demonstrates the power of regular contributions and dollar-cost averaging. Even with smaller, consistent investments, investors can reap significant rewards in the long run, thanks to the magic of compounding. The story of Jack and Jill serves as a reminder that consistency and patience often trump large, one-time investments when it comes to long-term wealth creation.

Tax Efficiency and Compounding

Tax efficiency and compounding are powerful concepts in the world of finance that can significantly impact your investment returns over time. Let's break down these concepts with a clear example:

Tax efficiency involves structuring your investments in a way that minimizes the amount of taxes you need to pay on your investment gains. By optimizing your investment strategy, you can legally reduce the impact of taxes on your overall returns.

Imagine you have two investment options: a taxable investment account and a tax-advantaged retirement account like a Roth IRA. In the taxable account, you invest in stocks and earn a 10% annual return. In the Roth IRA, you also invest in stocks and earn the same 10% annual return.

However, in the taxable account, you're subject to capital gains taxes on your investment gains, let's say, at a rate of 20%. In contrast, the Roth IRA allows your investments to grow tax-free, meaning you won't owe any taxes on your gains when you withdraw the money in retirement.

After 30 years, your initial investment of $10,000 in both accounts has grown to $174,494 due to the power of compounding. However, in the taxable account, you need to pay 20% in capital gains taxes on your gains, leaving you with $139,595.

In the Roth IRA, you get to keep the entire $174,494 since you don't owe any taxes on your gains. The tax efficiency of the Roth IRA has allowed you to retain more of your investment gains, resulting in a significant difference in your final account balance.

Let's take the same scenario with the Roth IRA and look at the compounding effect. You initially invest $10,000 and earn a 10% annual return. After the first year, your investment grows to $11,000. In the second year, you earn 10% on the $11,000, resulting in a gain of $1,100. This brings your total investment to $12,100.

As time goes on, the growth becomes more significant. After 30 years, your initial $10,000 investment has grown to $174,494, with the vast majority of the growth occurring in the later years due to the compounding effect. Compounding allows your investment gains to snowball, leading to substantial wealth accumulation over time.

When you combine tax efficiency with the compounding effect, the results can be even more remarkable. By minimizing the taxes, you pay on your investment gains; you're able to keep more of your earnings, allowing them to compound more effectively.

In the example above, if you had invested in the Roth IRA and maximized your tax advantages, your investment growth would have been even more significant due to the compounding effect of working on a larger base. Over decades, the synergy between tax efficiency and compounding can lead to substantial differences in your investment outcomes.

Thus, understanding and harnessing the power of tax efficiency and compounding can have a profound impact on your long-term financial success. By making smart investment decisions that consider both of these factors, you can optimize your returns and build wealth more effectively over time.

↗ Limitations of Compounding

Although compounding is indeed powerful, investing still comes with risks. Remember, while compounding can lead to exponential growth, it can also lead to exponential losses if the investment value declines.

For instance, suppose you invest in a stock that unfortunately decreases in value by 20% in the first year. If the stock's value drops by another 20% in the following year, the decline's impact is compounded, leading to more significant overall losses. This is because the second decrease is not just calculated on the original investment amount but also on the losses incurred during the first year. This can result in a compounded loss, decreasing the initial investment value even further.

This highlights the necessity of taking a balanced approach to investing, one that considers potential rewards and risks. Diversification, or spreading investments across a variety of assets or asset classes, can help manage this risk. Diversification can mitigate potential losses in one area with gains in another, providing a level of protection against the volatility of financial markets.

Therefore, while compounding can work wonders for an investor's portfolio when investments are performing well, you must understand and manage the risks involved. Recognizing that compounding can also amplify losses will help investors make more informed decisions and develop a more resilient investment strategy.

↗ Psychology and Investing: Navigating Cognitive Biases for Better Decision Making

What does psychology have to do with compounding? Well, compounding's worst enemy is emotions. Selling for the wrong reason or not reinvesting will damage your compounding power.

Understanding Behavioural Finance

In the world of finance and investing, psychology plays a critical role. Every decision to buy, hold, or sell a security is influenced, to varying degrees, by emotional and cognitive biases. Understanding these influences is a core aspect of behavioural finance—a field that blends psychological insights with conventional economic and financial theory to predict investment outcomes.

The Influence of Present Bias on Investment Decisions

One concept in behavioural finance that stands out is 'present bias', a cognitive bias where individuals give more weight to immediate rewards at the expense of future gains. An apt analogy would be myopia or shortsightedness, where distant objects appear blurry while nearby items are in sharp focus. In investment terms, investors may be so focused on the short-term fluctuations in the market that they lose sight of their long-term investment strategy.

Present bias can significantly influence decision-making in investing. For example, it can lead investors to make impulsive buying decisions based on current market trends rather than long-term value. It may also cause them to overvalue the immediate perceived loss of selling a losing investment over the potential future losses.

Managing Cognitive Biases in Investing

Overcoming cognitive biases, including present bias, is no easy task, as these biases are deeply ingrained in our decision-making processes. However, awareness and recognition of these biases is the first step towards better decision-making. Below are some of the common cognitive biases that can affect investment decisions:

1. **Egocentric Bias:** People tend to believe that their thoughts and actions are more common and correct than they actually are. This bias may lead investors to overestimate their investment prowess or the quality of their information.

2. **Equity Bias:** This bias refers to the tendency to perceive fairness based on one's own situation. An investor might perceive a high-risk, high-return investment as fair, while others might view it as disproportionately risky.

3. **Endowment Effect:** People often value things they own more than those they don't. In investing, this can manifest as holding onto an underperforming stock because you own it and overvalue it, even if its prospects are poor.

4. **Hot-Cold Empathy Gap:** This refers to the tendency to underestimate the influence of emotional states on decision-making. An investor might make risky decisions when in a 'hot' emotional state, like euphoria after a market upswing, that they wouldn't consider in a 'cold,' or calm, state.

5. **Loss Aversion:** The pain of losing is psychologically about twice as potent as the pleasure of gaining, leading investors to avoid selling a losing investment to prevent the emotional pain of realizing a loss.

6. **Hyperbolic Discounting:** Investors with this bias prefer smaller, immediate payoffs over larger, future ones,

leading to short-term investment decisions at the expense of long-term gains.

The impact of these cognitive biases can be mitigated by adopting a disciplined and structured approach to investing. Regularly reviewing and assessing your portfolio, taking a long-term perspective, diversifying investments, and not getting swayed by short-term market trends can help in managing these biases.

A key strategy could be to consistently ask yourself, 'Would I buy this stock at its current price?' If the answer is 'no', consider selling it. If 'yes', it might be worth holding onto it. This approach forces you to continuously re-evaluate the worth of your holdings based on their current market value, not just the price at which you bought them.

The Most Influential Biases on Decision-Making

- **Illusion of Skill:** We regularly confuse luck with skill because we solely focus on outcomes.

- **Recency Bias:** We tend to put too much weight on recent events.

- **Anchoring:** Our judgment is heavily skewed by the first information we are given about something.

- **Regression:** We love to see cause-effect relationships where none exist. Everything, always, regresses to its mean!

- **Hindsight Bias:** In retrospect, events seem more predictable than they were.

- **Halo Effect:** You either like or dislike everything about someone or something. Nothing in between.

- **Loss Aversion:** Losses weigh twice as much as the equivalent gain. Because of that, we reject gambles where chance would favour us.

- **Commitment Bias:** We tend to remain committed to our past behaviours and opinions. Particularly when expressed publicly, even if they do not have desirable outcomes.

- **WYSIATI:** What you see is all there is. You can't consider what you don't know. Paradoxically, knowing less also increases your confidence about being right.

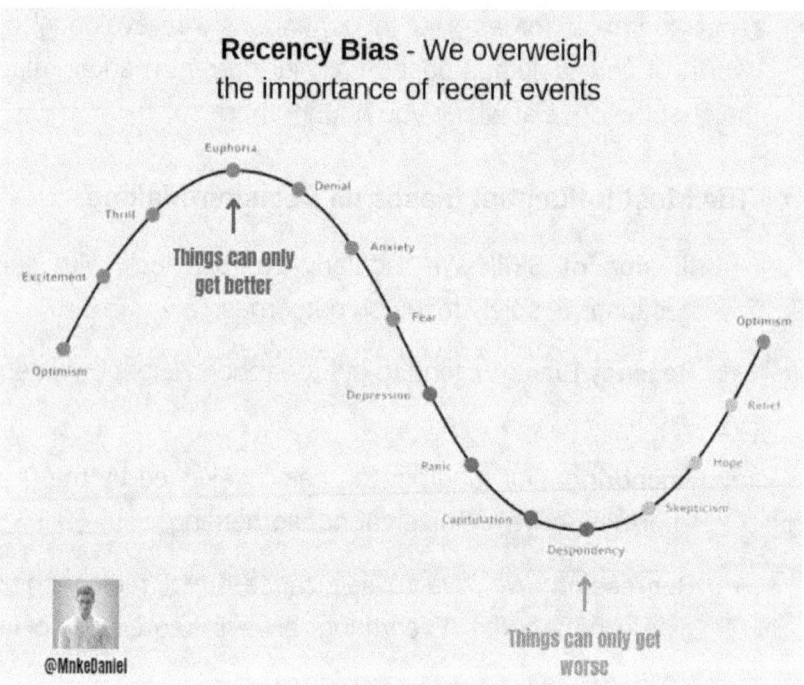

Understanding psychology and its impact on investment decision-making is crucial for successful investing. By recognizing the cognitive biases that impact investment decisions, investors can better manage their responses to market movements, make more informed choices, and enhance their overall investment performance. One of the greatest challenges of investing is managing one's own emotions and biases. Hence, the key to successful investing often lies as much in understanding oneself as it does in understanding the markets.

Strategies such as rebalancing the portfolio periodically and seeking advice from a financial advisor can also provide a system of checks and balances to ensure our biases don't lead us astray. Financial advisors can provide an objective perspective, free from the cognitive biases that the investor might be subject to. Ultimately, effective investing is not just about picking the right stocks or timing the market perfectly but also about navigating the complex terrain of human psychology. As legendary investor Benjamin Graham once said, 'The investor's chief problem—and even his worst enemy—is likely to be himself.'

↗ Conclusion

As we reach the end of this chapter, I invite you to take a moment and reflect on what we've discovered about the incredible power of compounding. This phenomenon is more than just a financial concept; it's a tool that you can leverage on your wealth creation journey.

Imagine what your future could look like if you harness the power of compounding. Could it help you reach your financial goals more quickly? Would it change the way you think about investing and managing your money? Remember the examples of Coca-Cola, Microsoft, Apple, and Visa. Consider how the compounding effect has helped many patient and disciplined investors accumulate substantial wealth over time.

At the same time, remember the risk-return trade-off. As you've seen, while compounding can lead to significant growth, it can also amplify losses if not managed correctly. Developing a balanced and diversified investment strategy can help you navigate these risks while capitalizing on the opportunities compounding offers.

As we move forward, consider how understanding compounding can influence your investment decisions. Remember, the power to create wealth lies not just in the amount you invest but also in the time you allow your investments to grow. Starting early, reinvesting dividends, and remaining patient can yield impressive results over time.

In conclusion, I hope that you use the knowledge gained in this chapter not only to understand compounding but also to leverage its power in your wealth-creation journey. The decision to embrace the magic of compounding can set you on a path toward financial success and help you achieve your long-term wealth goals.

KEY TAKEAWAYS

- Compounding transforms small investments into substantial wealth over time, emphasizing the importance of starting early and remaining patient.

- Reinvesting dividends through plans like DRIP accelerates compounding growth.

- Combining compounding with tax optimization enhances long-term returns.

- Considering the trade-off between risk and return, diversification and sound strategies mitigate risk.

- Dollar-cost averaging with regular investments capitalizes on market fluctuations.

- Awareness of biases in decision-making, like present bias, is crucial for better investment choices. Managing emotions and biases is as important as understanding market trends.

CHAPTER 9

BUILDING A PORTFOLIO WITH OPTIMAL PORTFOLIO DIVERSIFICATION

"In investing, what is comfortable
it is rarely profitable."

– Robert Arnott

Have you ever experienced significant losses in your investment portfolio due to a single investment's poor performance? Have you ever encountered situations where your investments in a particular industry or sector were affected by unforeseen events? If you have encountered such situations, the next question you will ask is, 'Is there a way of balancing potential returns and risk in your investment portfolio?' Well, certainly, yes, through diversification of your portfolio.

Understanding the importance of diversification in portfolio management is crucial for any investor. Investors can reduce risk and optimize potential returns by spreading investments across various assets and sectors. This chapter aims to guide readers in creating a diversified investment portfolio, exploring the factors influencing diversification decisions, and introducing strategies for achieving optimal diversification.

↗ Understanding Portfolio Diversification

Diversification is a key concept in portfolio management that involves spreading investments across different assets to minimize risk. It helps to mitigate losses from poor-performing investments and take advantage of opportunities in various market sectors. Investors can create a well-balanced and stable portfolio by allocating investments across different asset classes, such as stocks, bonds, real estate and commodities. When selecting individual securities to enhance diversification, it's important to consider factors like market capitalization, investment style and geographic location. While diversification can reduce risk, it doesn't guarantee profits or protect against all losses, so thorough research, analysis and monitoring are crucial for maintaining an optimal diversified portfolio.

While there isn't a specific mathematical formula for portfolio diversification itself, several measures can be used to assess the level of diversification in a portfolio.

Correlation Coefficient: The correlation coefficient measures the relationship between the returns of two assets. It is calculated using the formula:

$$\rho(X, Y) = \text{cov}(X, Y) / (\sigma X * \sigma Y)$$

Where:
$\rho(X, Y)$ represents the correlation coefficient between assets X and Y.
$\text{cov}(X, Y)$ represents the covariance between assets X and Y.
σX represents the standard deviation of asset X's returns.
σY represents the standard deviation of asset Y's returns.

Investors can achieve better diversification by selecting assets with low or negative correlations. The correlation coefficient can take values between -1 and 1. A correlation coefficient of -1 indicates a perfect negative correlation, meaning that the returns of the two assets move in opposite directions. A correlation coefficient of 0 indicates no correlation, implying that the returns of the two assets are independent of each other. The movements in one asset's returns do not have any impact on the other asset's returns. A correlation coefficient of 1 indicates a perfect positive correlation, meaning that the returns of the two assets move in the same direction. This implies that when one asset's return increases, the other asset's return increases by the same magnitude.

By selecting assets with low or negative correlations (close to -1 or 0), investors can achieve better diversification. This is because assets with low correlations tend to have different

Building a Portfolio with Optimal Portfolio Diversification

price movements, reducing the impact of any single asset's poor performance on the overall portfolio.

Beta: Beta is a measure of an asset's sensitivity to market movements. Investors can diversify their portfolios by selecting assets with different betas and reducing systematic risk. It is calculated using the following formula:

$\beta = cov(X, M) / var(M)$

Where:
β represents the beta of the asset X.
$cov(X, M)$ represents the covariance between the asset X and the market.
$var(M)$ represents the variance of the market returns.

A beta greater than 1 indicates that the asset is more volatile than the market, while a beta less than 1 indicates that the asset is less volatile than the market.

Sharpe Ratio: The Sharpe ratio is a measure of risk-adjusted return. A higher Sharpe ratio indicates better risk-adjusted performance and can be used to assess the diversification benefits of a portfolio. It is calculated using the following formula:

Sharpe Ratio = $(R_p - R_f) / \sigma_p$

Where:
Sharpe Ratio represents the calculated Sharpe ratio.
R_p represents the expected portfolio return.
R_f represents the risk-free rate of return.
σ_p represents the portfolio standard deviation.

The Sharpe ratio indicates the excess return generated per unit of risk taken. A higher Sharpe ratio implies better risk-adjusted performance.

Portfolio Variance: Portfolio variance measures a portfolio's overall variability of returns. It takes into account the weights, variances and correlations of individual assets. The formula for portfolio variance is:

$$\text{Portfolio Variance} = [(w_1^2 * \sigma_1^2) + (w_2^2 * \sigma_2^2) + 2 * w_1 * w_2 * \rho_{12} * \sigma_1 * \sigma_2 + \ldots + (w_n^2 * \sigma_n^2) + 2 * \sum\sum (w_i * w_j * \rho_{ij} * \sigma_i * \sigma_j)]$$

Where:
$w_1, w_2, \ldots, w_n$ = Weights of the individual assets in the portfolio
$\sigma_1, \sigma_2, \ldots, \sigma_n$ = Standard deviations of the individual assets
$\rho_{12}, \rho_{13}, \ldots, \rho_{ij}$ = Correlations between the individual assets

To calculate portfolio risk, investors typically use the standard deviation, which quantifies the variability of returns. This involves considering the individual asset risks and correlations between assets.

Here are the formulas for portfolio risk:

Portfolio Standard Deviation:
$$\text{Portfolio Standard Deviation} = \sqrt{[(w_1^2 * \sigma_1^2) + (w_2^2 * \sigma_2^2) + 2 * w_1 * w_2 * \rho_{12} * \sigma_1 * \sigma_2 + \ldots + (w_n^2 * \sigma_n^2) + 2 * \sum\sum (w_i * w_j * \rho_{ij} * \sigma_i * \sigma_j)]}$$

Portfolio Variance:
$$\text{Portfolio Variance} = [(w_1^2 * \sigma_1^2) + (w_2^2 * \sigma_2^2) + 2 * w_1 * w_2 * \rho_{12} * \sigma_1 * \sigma_2 + \ldots + (w_n^2 * \sigma_n^2) + 2 * \sum\sum (w_i * w_j * \rho_{ij} * \sigma_i * \sigma_j)]$$

It's important to note that while these formulas help evaluate the diversification and risk of a portfolio, the selection of assets and the consideration of risk-return trade-offs play a crucial role in effective portfolio diversification. Measures and formulas provide quantitative assessment, but the art of diversification lies in constructing a well-balanced portfolio that aligns with an investor's risk tolerance and investment goals.

↗ Factors Influencing Diversification Decisions

Several factors play a significant role in influencing diversification decisions when constructing an investment portfolio. Understanding these factors is essential for making informed decisions that align with an investor's risk tolerance, investment horizon, financial goals, and overall economic environment. Let's delve deeper into these key factors.

Risk Tolerance

Every investor has a unique risk tolerance, which reflects their ability to withstand fluctuations in the value of their investments. Some investors may be more comfortable with higher levels of risk, while others prefer a more conservative approach. Risk tolerance is influenced by factors such as financial circumstances, investment knowledge and personal preferences. When considering diversification, it's important to ensure that the portfolio aligns with the investor's risk tolerance, striking a balance between potential returns and risk exposure.

Investment Horizon

The investment horizon refers to the length of time an investor plans to hold their investments before needing to access the funds. Investors with longer time horizons, such as those saving for retirement or long-term financial goals, may have a higher tolerance for short-term volatility and can potentially consider a more aggressive diversification strategy. Conversely, investors with shorter time horizons, such as those saving for a near-term expense, may prioritize capital preservation and opt for a more conservative diversification approach.

Financial Goals

Investors have various financial goals, such as capital preservation, income generation, or capital appreciation. The diversification strategy should align with these. For example, an investor focused on generating income may include dividend-paying stocks or bonds in their portfolio. In contrast, an investor seeking long-term growth may allocate a larger portion of their portfolio to equities. Diversification decisions should reflect the specific objectives and desired outcomes of each investor.

Economic Environment

The overall economic environment, including factors such as interest rates, inflation and market conditions, can greatly influence diversification decisions. Different sectors and asset classes perform differently under various economic conditions. For instance, during periods of economic expansion, certain sectors like technology or consumer discretionary may outperform, while defensive sectors like utilities or consumer staples may be more resilient during economic downturns. Understanding the current economic landscape helps investors identify potential opportunities and risks and adjust their diversification strategy accordingly.

By considering these factors, investors can make informed decisions when diversifying their portfolios. It is crucial to strike a balance between risk and reward, tailoring the diversification strategy to individual circumstances and investment objectives. A comprehensive understanding of risk tolerance, investment horizon, financial goals and the economic environment lays the foundation for constructing a well-diversified portfolio.

↗ Strategies for Achieving Optimal Diversification

Achieving optimal portfolio diversification requires various strategies that help spread investments across different assets and sectors. Each strategy aims to strike a balance between risk reduction and potential returns. Let's explore some of the key strategies for achieving optimal portfolio diversification.

Asset Allocation

Asset allocation involves determining the ideal mix of asset classes within a portfolio. This strategy considers the investor's risk tolerance, investment goals and time horizon. By diversifying across various asset classes, such as stocks, bonds, real estate and commodities, investors can reduce the risk associated with any single asset class. The allocation of assets within the portfolio can be adjusted over time to maintain the desired level of diversification.

Sector Diversification

Sector diversification involves spreading investments across different industry sectors. Industries can perform differently based on economic conditions, market trends and regulatory changes. Investing in sectors with a low correlation to one another can reduce the impact of any one sector's underperformance on the overall portfolio. Sector diversification also allows investors to capitalize on opportunities in sectors experiencing growth or having favourable prospects.

Geographical Diversification

Geographical diversification involves investing in different countries or regions. Economic conditions, political stability and regulatory environments vary significantly across geographies. By spreading investments globally, investors can reduce the impact of country-specific risks and take advantage of growth opportunities in different regions.

Diversification Across Investment Styles

Diversification across investment styles involves balancing investments between growth-oriented and value-oriented securities. Growth-oriented investments focus on companies with high growth potential, while value-oriented investments focus on undervalued assets with the potential for appreciation. By combining growth and value investments, investors can diversify their exposure to different market trends and investment philosophies, reducing the impact of any single investment style's performance.

It's important to note that each diversification strategy has its advantages and disadvantages, and their suitability may vary depending on an investor's specific circumstances and goals. These strategies should be selected and implemented based on thorough research, analysis, and consideration of individual risk profiles.

To achieve optimal diversification, investors should regularly review and rebalance their portfolios. This involves periodically assessing the performance of different assets, sectors and geographic regions and adjusting to maintain the desired level of diversification. Rebalancing helps ensure that the portfolio remains aligned with the investor's risk tolerance and investment objectives, especially as market conditions change over time.

↗ Building a Diversified Portfolio: Step-by-Step

Building a diversified portfolio involves a systematic approach that encompasses several key steps. By following these steps, investors can construct a portfolio that aligns with their risk tolerance, investment goals and desired level of diversification.

Here is a step-by-step guide to building a diversified portfolio.

Define Investment Goals and Risk Tolerance

Start by clearly defining your investment goals and understanding your risk tolerance. Consider factors such as your financial objectives, time horizon and comfort level with market fluctuations. This step lays the foundation for determining the appropriate level of diversification.

Determine Asset Allocation

Determine the ideal asset allocation for your portfolio. This involves deciding how much of your portfolio should be allocated to different asset classes, such as stocks, bonds, real estate and cash. Consider your risk tolerance, investment goals and the expected returns and risks associated with each asset class.

Select Specific Securities or Investment Products

Once you have determined your asset allocation, select specific securities or investment products within each asset class. Conduct thorough research on individual stocks, bonds, mutual funds, exchange-traded funds (ETFs) or other investment vehicles. Consider factors such as company fundamentals, credit ratings, expense ratios and historical performance.

Rebalance the Portfolio

Regularly review and rebalance your portfolio to maintain the desired level of diversification. Rebalancing involves adjusting the portfolio's allocation by buying or selling assets to align with your target asset allocation. This ensures that your portfolio doesn't become too heavily weighted towards any specific asset class or investment.

Monitor and Review Portfolio Performance

Continuously monitor and review the performance of your portfolio. Keep track of how individual investments are performing relative to their benchmarks and the overall market. Regularly assess the portfolio's performance against your investment goals and risk tolerance. Make adjustments as necessary to optimize your portfolio's diversification and align it with changing market conditions.

Surviving the tumultuous 2008 financial crisis was no easy feat, but those embracing diversification were better equipped to weather the storm. By spreading investments across different asset classes, sectors and regions, diversified portfolios could mitigate risks and cushion the blow. This strategy provided a crucial defence against systemic risk, helped navigate market volatility, capitalized on unique opportunities and ultimately taught investors a valuable lesson about the importance of diversification in managing risk and pursuing long-term success.

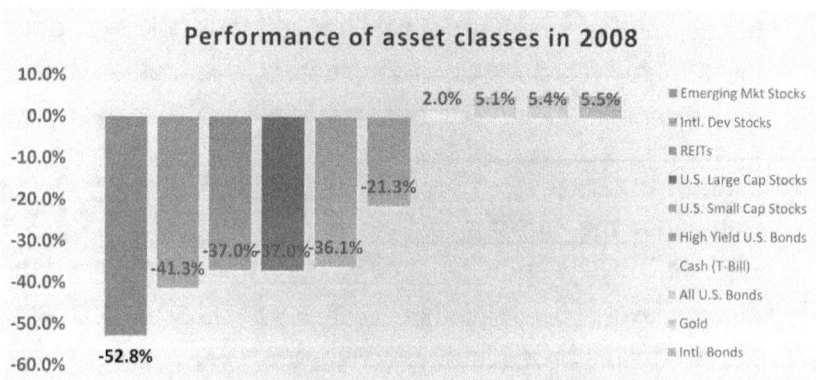

Source: Figures taken from https://www.visualcapitalist.com/historical-returns-by-asset-class/

Let's look at an example to understand how portfolio diversification would have helped investors to reduce their losses during the 2008 financial crisis, which shocked the global financial markets.

Assets	2008 Performance	Portfolio 1	Portfolio 2	Portfolio 3
U.S. Large Cap Stocks	-37.0%	60%	60%	30%
Cash (T-Bill)	2.0%	-	-	20%
REITs	-37.0%	-	40%	20%
All U.S. Bonds	5.1%	-	-	20%
Gold	5.4%	-	-	10%
U.S. Small Cap Stocks	-36.1%	40%	-	-
		100%	100%	100%
	Portfolio Return (%)	-36.64%	-37.00%	-16.54%

You can see in the example that Portfolio 2, consisting of U.S. Large Cap Stocks and REITs, performed worst at -37%, whereas Portfolio 1, consisting of U.S. large and small-cap stocks, too, performed similarly at -36.64%. On the other hand, Portfolio 3, which was much diversified across different asset classes from large and small stocks to REITs, bonds, and cash, performed better among the three with -16.54%.

It is important to understand that when asset classes performed drastically lower, with 35 to 40% down, to have a portfolio on diversified lines giving only -16.54% return can be said to have performed better.

Now, how open are you to exploring the concept of diversification? Are you comfortable with the idea of investing in assets that have different patterns of growth and decline? Would you consider diversifying your investments to manage this variability? If so, try the Portfolio Visualizer tool that allows users to input various assets (stocks, bonds, ETFs) to see how diversified their portfolio is and how it might perform under different market conditions.

↗ Examples of Diversified Portfolios

Let's explore some examples of well-diversified portfolios to provide a practical understanding of how diversification can be implemented. These examples showcase different strategies and asset allocations, offering insights into how investors can achieve optimal diversification.

Example 1: The Balanced Portfolio

A balanced portfolio is designed to provide a mix of growth and income while maintaining a moderate level of risk. It typically includes a diversified blend of stocks, bonds and cash equivalents. For instance, a balanced portfolio might allocate 60% to stocks, 30% to bonds and 10% to cash or money market funds.

Within the stock allocation, the portfolio may include a mix of large-cap, mid-cap and small-cap stocks across various sectors such as technology, healthcare, consumer goods and finance. The bond portion might consist of government, corporate and municipal bonds with different maturities and credit ratings. This combination allows the portfolio to benefit from potential stock market growth while providing stability through income-generating fixed-income investments.

Example 2: The Global Portfolio

A global portfolio aims to capture opportunities across different regions and economies. It seeks diversification by investing in companies and assets from around the world. For instance, the portfolio may allocate a significant portion to U.S. equities, considering the size and stability of the U.S. market. It may also include allocations to emerging markets, such as China, India and Brazil, to benefit from their growth potential.

A global portfolio may also include exposure to internationally developed markets like Europe and Japan, which provide opportunities in established industries and global brands. By diversifying geographically, the portfolio can reduce the risk associated with country-specific events and take advantage of growth and stability in different regions.

Example 3: The Sector-Focused Portfolio

A sector-focused portfolio aims to capitalize on specific industry trends or themes. It concentrates investments in sectors expected to outperform or have long-term growth prospects. For instance, a sector-focused portfolio may allocate a significant portion to technology stocks, benefiting from innovation, digital transformation and technological advancements.

This portfolio may also include allocations to other sectors with favourable prospects, such as healthcare, clean energy, or consumer discretionary. By concentrating investments in sectors with strong growth potential, the portfolio seeks to outperform the broader market. However, investors should be mindful of the higher risk associated with sector-focused strategies, as they are susceptible to sector-specific risks and volatility.

These examples illustrate how different strategies can be implemented to achieve diversification. Investors can adopt these approaches by considering their risk tolerance, investment goals and market conditions. It is important to conduct thorough research, assess individual investments, and regularly monitor and rebalance the portfolio to ensure it remains properly diversified and aligned with the investor's objectives.

Over-Diversification: A Word of Caution

While diversification is generally beneficial, over-diversification can present challenges and potentially hinder portfolio performance. Over-diversification occurs when a portfolio becomes excessively fragmented or diluted, resulting in reduced potential returns and increased complexity in portfolio management. Here's a more detailed explanation of the issues associated with over-diversification.

Dilution of Potential Returns

When a portfolio is over-diversified, the impact of individual high-performing investments may be diminished. While diversification helps mitigate risks, it can also limit the potential upside of concentrated investments that could have generated significant returns. By spreading investments too thin across numerous holdings, the overall portfolio may experience mediocre returns, lacking the impact of standout performers.

Difficulty in Portfolio Management

Managing an over-diversified portfolio can become challenging and time-consuming. With a large number of holdings, it becomes more complex to monitor and analyse each investment's performance, financial health and industry dynamics. Investors may find it difficult to stay updated on company news, earnings reports and market trends for each holding. Consequently, portfolio management may become less efficient and potentially hinder the ability to make timely investment decisions.

Increased Costs

Over-diversification can lead to higher costs associated with managing the portfolio. Each additional holding requires due diligence, research and potential transaction fees. As the number of holdings increases, these costs can accumulate, eroding potential returns. Additionally, the increased complexity may necessitate the use of investment vehicles such as mutual funds or ETFs, which have their own expenses, including management fees.

Loss of Focus and Expertise

When a portfolio becomes excessively diversified, it becomes challenging for investors to understand each holding and its underlying fundamentals. Investors may lose focus and fail to stay informed about specific industries or sectors. This lack of expertise can hinder the ability to make informed investment decisions and capitalize on opportunities that require specialized knowledge.

To illustrate the potential drawbacks of over-diversification, let's consider a real stock example:

Suppose an investor holds a portfolio with excessive stocks, each representing a very small percentage of the total portfolio value. While this approach aims to reduce risk by diversifying across numerous stocks, it can lead to diluted returns. For instance, if the portfolio consists of 100 stocks, each representing only 1% of its value, even if a few stocks perform exceptionally well, their positive impact on the overall portfolio may be limited due to their small weighting. As a result, the potential returns of these standout performers may not significantly impact the overall portfolio's performance.

It's important to note that the specific stocks and their performance will vary based on market conditions and individual holdings. However, the general principle of diluting potential returns due to over-diversification applies across various stock examples.

To avoid over-diversification, investors should strike a balance between diversification and concentration. They should focus on quality investments, ensure that each holding contributes meaningfully to the portfolio's risk and return profile, and avoid excessive duplication of holdings. Regular portfolio monitoring and analysis can help identify areas of potential over-diversification and allow for adjustments to maintain an optimal level of diversification.

How to Avoid or Deal with Over-Diversification

Dealing with over-diversification, where an investment portfolio holds too many assets, can be as important as diversifying in the first place. Here's how to manage it:

Assess your portfolio's goals: Clarify your investment objectives and risk tolerance.

Understand your holdings: Know your investments intimately. Understand their strengths and weaknesses and how they fit into your overall strategy.

Streamline your holdings: Identify redundant or highly correlated assets. Trim holdings that don't contribute significantly to your portfolio's goals.

Focus on quality: Prioritize high-quality assets over quantity. Quality investments are more likely to deliver desirable returns and withstand market fluctuations.

Create a core portfolio: Build a core of essential investments that align with your long-term strategy. This can simplify management and reduce over-diversification.

Consider asset allocation: Allocate assets based on your goals, risk tolerance and time horizon. A well-thought-out allocation reduces the need for excessive diversification.

Avoid 'diworsification': Adding too many assets can dilute potential gains and increase complexity. Ensure each addition genuinely enhances your portfolio.

Regularly review and rebalance: Periodically assess your portfolio's performance and alignment with your goals. Adjust your holdings as needed to maintain balance.

Seek professional advice: Financial advisors can analyse your portfolio objectively and provide guidance on optimizing your investments.

Stay informed: Keep up with market trends and economic indicators. Being informed helps you make strategic decisions about your investments.

Remember, the goal is a balanced portfolio that aligns with your financial objectives while avoiding the unnecessary complexity that over-diversification can bring.

Practical examples:

'Don't look for the needle in the haystack. Just buy the haystack!' –John C. Bogle

---

Diversification doesn't have to be a chore—it can be your investment superpower. The simplest route? An index fund. It's the straightforward, time-tested strategy lauded in countless investing manuals. Sure, it might not be the most exhilarating option, but it's effective.

Want to step it up a notch? Consider an investment in a conglomerate like Berkshire Hathaway, but keep a sharp eye on the price tag—you're after value, not overpaying for a name.

Craving more diversification? Look globally. Multinational corporations operate across borders, diluting the impact of regional downturns or unexpected events—providing you with a buffer against localized economic tremors.

For those with a taste for the game and a hunger for higher stakes, small-cap investing might just be your calling. This is where you can play the field, backing the underdogs and potential disruptors. It's the realm where one standout performer can redefine your portfolio's success story. So go ahead, pick your champions and root for them—after all, in the investment arena, spotting the next star can be the golden ticket.

KEY TAKEAWAYS

- Diversification is crucial in portfolio management, reducing risk by spreading investments across assets and sectors.

- Factors like risk tolerance, investment horizon and financial goals impact diversification decisions.

- Asset diversification, sector diversification, geographical diversification and diversification across investment styles are a few methodologies for portfolio diversification.

- Understanding measures like the correlation coefficient, beta, Sharpe ratio and portfolio variance helps assess diversification levels.

- Over-diversification can dilute returns, increase complexity and hinder portfolio management.

- To avoid over-diversification, focus on quality, streamline holdings and seek professional advice, if needed.

- Building a diversified portfolio involves setting goals, selecting assets and regular monitoring.

- Striking a balance between diversification and concentration is key to achieving optimal results.

CHAPTER 10

THE FINAL VERDICT – UNRAVELING THE INVESTING PARADOX

The Final Verdict – Unraveling the Investing Paradox

Investing is a vast, complex ocean filled with a myriad of possibilities. Every investor embarks on their journey equipped with their unique financial goals, risk tolerance and investment knowledge. Throughout this book, we have unearthed the tales of various investing giants, behemoth companies and even some unexpected outperformers from the animal kingdom to Wall Street's dartboards.

If there's one crucial thing we've learned, it's that there is no 'one size fits all' strategy for investing. From the conservative approaches of Warren Buffett to the active management prowess of David Swensen, and the serendipitous success of Grace Groner's single-stock investment, the paths to financial prosperity are as diverse as the investors themselves.

The churning financial markets, driven by economic cycles, hold the potential to be a source of wealth creation, yet they demand a blend of strategic acumen and humble acceptance of the inherent risk. Passive investing and active investing are two sides of the same coin, each with distinct merits and limitations. As investors, we must understand these nuances to make informed decisions about our preferred investment style. However, the secret sauce to the investment success story isn't merely about choosing growth or value investing or even having the perfect blend of large-cap or small-cap stocks in your portfolio. The most common thread that weaves through all successful investment narratives is time.

Time is a steadfast ally in the world of investing, an elixir that magnifies the effect of compounding. The saga of Grace Groner is a testament to the adage – 'Time in the market is more important than timing the market.' When combined with a well-diversified portfolio, the ticking clock can transmute even modest investments into substantial wealth. Yet, while time is a potent element, successful investing also demands a deep understanding of what you're putting your money into. Just as the fall of Enron underscored the significance of robust corporate governance, so our investing choices should always be backed by diligent research. This knowledge empowers us to survive the market's inevitable downturns and capitalize on the opportunities they present.

On the flip side, let's not forget that investing isn't merely a numbers game. It's a discipline that tests our emotional resilience and decision-making abilities under pressure. As the unexpected success of the monkeys and the brain-damaged investors reveal, the secret to superior investment performance sometimes lies in freeing ourselves from the shackles of overthinking and fear. A certain degree of detachment and acceptance of uncertainty can be surprisingly advantageous.

But here's the ultimate paradox – even as we advocate for a calm and calculated approach to investing, remember that some of the most successful investments have been the result of seemingly random choices. Like the monkeys outperforming the market with their dartboards, or a certain cat named Orlando beating professional fund managers, the unpredictability of markets has a way of humbling even the most sophisticated of investors. This brings us to an essential realization – the world of investing is vast and diverse, with room for an array of strategies and approaches. From passive indexing to active stock picking, from following tried-and-true principles of corporate governance to betting on random selections, the right strategy is often one that resonates with you and aligns with your financial goals and risk tolerance.

One need only look at the varied success stories in the investing world to understand this. David Swensen, Warren Buffet, and even our non-human investors – the monkeys and the cat – each had a different approach. Yet, they all found success. Each story underscores that there isn't a one-size-fits-all blueprint for investing. Even as we embrace our individual investing paths, there are common threads that bind all successful investors. Patience, discipline and a keen understanding of risk and reward are universal investing virtues. The courage to be wrong, the humility to admit mistakes and the ability to learn from them are traits that every investor should aspire to cultivate.

Investing, at its core, is more than just about money. It's about harnessing the forces of time, compounding and market dynamics to create wealth. It's about making decisions under uncertainty and maintaining your composure when things don't go as planned. And more often than not, it's about simplicity and common sense rather than complex algorithms or sophisticated financial models. With knowledge, patience and the right mindset, you, too, can navigate this fascinating world, turning market turmoil into opportunities and uncertainties into stepping stones for success.

In the end, perhaps the most important investment you can make is in yourself – in your understanding of finance, in your ability to analyse and react to market events and in your capacity to maintain a long-term perspective even in the face of short-term market fluctuations. It is this investment, above all, that will stand you in good stead in the financial markets and beyond.

As we conclude this journey through the realm of investing, remember – the best investor is not the one who never makes mistakes but the one who learns from them. The most successful investor is not the one who avoids all risks but the one who understands them. And the wealthiest investor is not just the one with the most money but the one with the most wisdom. After all, in the game of investing, sometimes it's the player who enjoys the game the most that ends up winning. Happy investing!

BONUS CHAPTER

A FEW IMPORTANT COMPANY CASE HISTORIES AND QUOTES FROM LEGENDS

In this bonus section, we will delve into the intriguing case histories of real companies and analyse the profound impact of significant events on their stock performance. By examining the timelines of these companies and the corresponding changes in stock prices, we can derive valuable investing lessons that can shape our own investment strategies. These case histories underscore the critical importance of conducting thorough company analysis before making investment decisions, ensuring a comprehensive understanding of the factors that can influence a company's value.

↗ Case History: Apple Inc. (AAPL)

Timeline

- 1976: Apple was founded by Steve Jobs, Steve Wozniak and Ronald Wayne to bring user-friendly computers to the masses. The company went public in December 1980.

- 1984: Apple introduces the Macintosh computer, featuring a graphical user interface and a mouse, revolutionizing the personal computer industry. The launch of the Macintosh contributes to a surge in Apple's stock price, reflecting investors' optimism about the company's future prospects.

- 1997: Apple faces financial challenges and declining market share. Steve Jobs returns to the company as CEO, leading a successful turnaround and revitalizing Apple's product line. Jobs' leadership inspires renewed investor confidence, resulting in a gradual increase in Apple's stock price.

- 2001: Apple introduces the iPod, a portable digital music player. The iPod became a game-changer in the music industry and establishes Apple as a leader in consumer electronics. The introduction of the iPod contributes to a significant rise in Apple's stock price as investors recognize the company's potential for growth and market dominance.

- 2007: Apple launches the iPhone, a revolutionary smartphone that combines communication, internet access and multimedia capabilities. The iPhone becomes a global phenomenon, transforming the mobile phone industry and driving Apple's growth. The introduction of the iPhone triggers a substantial surge in Apple's stock price, as investors anticipated strong sales and increased revenue.

- 2010: Apple introduces the iPad, a tablet computer that creates a new market segment and further solidifies Apple's position as an innovator. The launch of the iPad results in a significant boost to Apple's stock price, reflecting investor optimism about the potential market demand for the new device.

- 2011: Steve Jobs passes away, leaving a lasting legacy of innovation and visionary leadership at Apple. Following Jobs' death, Apple's stock experiences a short-term decline as investors express concerns about its ability to maintain its innovative edge without its iconic leader.

- 2014: Apple enters the wearables market with the launch of the Apple Watch, expanding its product ecosystem and diversifying revenue streams. The release of the Apple Watch contributes to a moderate increase in Apple's stock price as investors recognize the company's efforts to expand beyond its traditional product categories.

- 2020: Apple becomes the first publicly traded company to reach a market capitalization of $2 trillion, reflecting its continued success and market dominance. This milestone triggers a surge in Apple's stock price, driven by investor confidence in the company's financial performance, strong product lineup, and loyal customer base.

Investing lessons

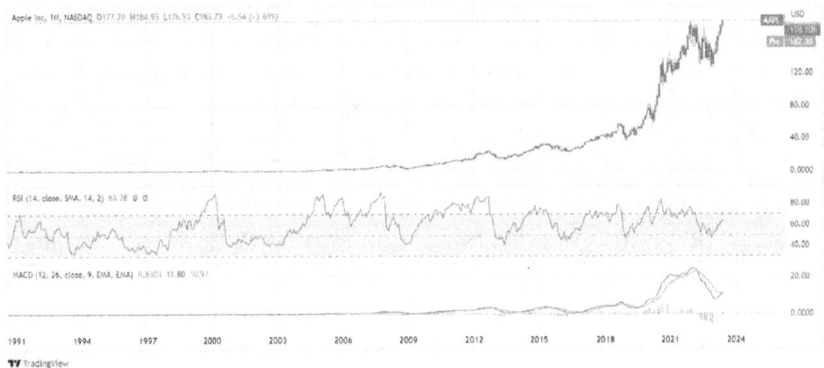

- Apple's case history showcases innovation's transformative power and visionary leadership's impact on stock performance. Throughout its journey, Apple has introduced groundbreaking products that have disrupted industries and captured the imagination of consumers worldwide. The successful launches of the Macintosh, iPod, iPhone, iPad and Apple Watch have generated significant revenue for Apple and driven its stock price to new heights.

- Innovation and differentiation are crucial for sustained success. Companies that can develop groundbreaking products and deliver unique value propositions have a higher chance of achieving long-term growth. These innovations can drive customer demand, revenue growth and positive stock price performance.

- Leadership is critical in shaping a company's direction and driving its success. Evaluating the leadership team's track record, vision and ability to execute is important when considering an investment in a company. Strong and visionary leadership, as demonstrated by Steve Jobs's return to Apple, can inspire investor confidence and positively impact stock performance.

- Diversification within a company's product portfolio can help mitigate risks and capture new growth opportunities. Apple's expansion into complementary markets, such as wearables with the Apple Watch, has enabled it to diversify its revenue streams and strengthen its overall position. This diversification can contribute to sustained stock price growth.

- Investors need to consider a company's competitive position, market trends and the potential for future innovation when evaluating long-term investment opportunities. Analysing a company's product pipeline and ability to adapt to changing consumer preferences can provide valuable insights into future growth prospects and stock price movements. Investors can learn valuable lessons from Apple's case history, including the importance of investing in companies with a strong culture of innovation, a track record of delivering innovative products, and a diversified product portfolio. By studying Apple's journey, investors can gain insights into the key drivers of success and make informed investment decisions in the dynamic technology sector. Additionally, analysing the relationship between significant events and stock price reactions can provide valuable insights into market dynamics and investor sentiment.

Case History: Enron Corporation

Timeline

- 1985: Enron is formed through the merger of Houston Natural Gas and InterNorth, positioning itself as a leading energy company. Enron's stock experiences steady growth in the following years.

- The late 1990s: Enron starts engaging in complex financial transactions and accounting practices, including off-balance-sheet partnerships. These practices allow Enron to hide debt and inflate its reported earnings, leading to an artificial boost in its stock price.

- 2001: Enron's deceptive accounting practices are exposed, and the company files for bankruptcy. The revelation of accounting fraud leads to a rapid decline in Enron's stock price, causing significant losses for investors.

Investing lessons

- Transparency and ethical business practices are crucial when evaluating potential investments. The Enron case highlights the importance of conducting thorough due diligence and examining a company's financial statements and disclosures to ensure accuracy and transparency.

- Understanding the risks associated with complex financial structures and accounting practices is essential. Investors should be cautious of companies that engage in overly complex transactions, as they can obscure the true financial health of the company and lead to significant losses when exposed.

- Diversification and risk management are critical in mitigating the impact of investment losses. By diversifying their portfolios across different industries and asset classes, investors can minimize the impact of any single company's failure on their overall investment performance.

↗ Case History: Tesla, Inc.

Timeline

- 2003: Tesla is founded to accelerate the world's transition to sustainable energy. The company initially focuses on developing electric vehicles (EVs) and battery technology.

- 2008: Tesla introduces the Tesla Roadster, the world's first all-electric sports car. While the Roadster's initial production is limited, it showcases Tesla's innovative technology and establishes the company as a pioneer in the EV market.

- 2010: Tesla goes public, offering its shares to the public. The IPO receives significant investor interest, and Tesla's stock price experiences initial volatility.

- 2012: Tesla launches the Model S, a fully electric luxury sedan that receives critical acclaim and establishes Tesla as a serious competitor in the automotive industry. Positive reviews and strong demand contribute to Tesla's stock price surge.

- 2014: Tesla plans to build a Gigafactory, a large-scale battery manufacturing plant. This strategic move aimed to address concerns about EV range and battery availability. The announcement positively impacts Tesla's stock price, as investors recognize its efforts to expand its manufacturing capabilities.

- 2020: Tesla becomes the world's most valuable automaker, surpassing traditional industry giants. The company's stock experienced a significant surge, driven by investor enthusiasm for Tesla's electric vehicles, energy products and its potential to disrupt the automotive industry.

Investing lessons

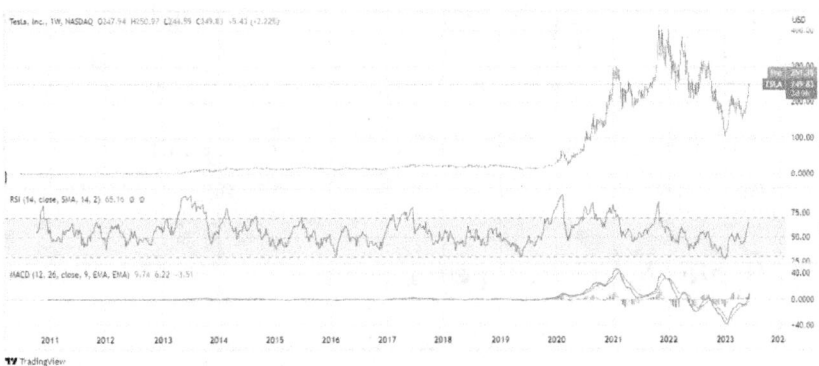

- Investing in companies at the forefront of technological innovation can yield significant returns. Tesla's case history highlights the potential for exponential growth when investing in disruptive industries and transformative technologies.

- Understanding the competitive landscape and market dynamics is crucial. Tesla's success is partly attributed to its ability to differentiate itself from traditional automakers and capitalize on the growing demand for sustainable transportation solutions.

- Evaluating a company's long-term vision, execution capabilities and management team is important when considering an investment. Tesla's case history underscores the significance of strong leadership and a clear strategic roadmap in driving sustained growth and investor confidence.

↗ Conclusion

The case histories of Apple, Enron and Tesla provide valuable insights into the dynamics of stock performance and the lessons investors can learn from the experiences of these companies. From the remarkable success of Apple, driven by innovation and visionary leadership, to the cautionary tales of Enron's corporate fraud and Tesla's journey in the electric vehicle industry, each case offers unique lessons that can guide investors in making informed investment decisions.

↗ Quotes from Investment Legends

Next in this chapter we have some snippets of wisdom and insight from marketing and investment legends. These quotes encapsulate years of experience, successful strategies, and valuable lessons that have shaped the worlds of marketing and investment. Get ready to be inspired and gain valuable knowledge from these visionary minds.

'Rule No. 1 is never to lose money.
Rule No. 2 is never forget Rule No. 1'.
– Warren Buffett

'If you invest $1,000 in a stock,
all you can lose is $1,000, but you stand to gain $10,000
or even $50,000 over time if you're patient.'
– Peter Lynch

'Investing can be very simple: buy good companies,
don't overpay and do nothing.'
– Terry Smith

'The secret to successful investing is relatively simple:
Figure out the value of something and then pay a lot less.'
– Joel Greenblatt

'In the short run, the market is a voting machine
but in the long run, it is a weighing machine.'
– Benjamin Graham

'Being a value investor means you look at the
downside before looking at the upside.'
– Li Lu

'If you want to become wealthy, you must
have your money work for you.'
– John Templeton

'Time is your friend; impulse is your enemy.'
– John Bogle

'You know, a balance sheet is like a bikini,
it shows more but it hides what is vital.'
– Rakesh Jhunjhunwala

'The big money is not in the buying or
selling but in the waiting.'
— Charlie Munger

If you are smart, you do not need leverage. If you
are not smart, you should not use it
— Warren Buffet

John Maynard Keynes famously stated, 'The market
can stay irrational longer than you can stay solvent.'

Anybody who doesn't change their mind a lot
is dramatically understimating the complexity
of the world that we live in
— Jeff Bezos

'Everyone has the brainpower to follow the stock market.
If you made it through fifth-grade math, you can do it.'
— Peter Lynch

'If you buy the same securities everyone else is buying,
you will have the same results as everyone else.'
— John Templeton

'Whether we're talking about socks or stocks, I like buying
quality merchandise when it is marked down.'
— Warren Buffett

'When a stock rises to, say, 50 or 60 or 70, per cent, the
urge to sell and take a profit now that the stock is "high"
becomes irresistible to many people. Giving in to this urge
can be very costly.'
— Philip Fisher

'Over the long-term, the miracle of compounding returns is overwhelmed by the tyranny of compounding cost.'
— John Bogle

'If you are shopping for common stocks, choose them the way you would buy groceries, not the way you would buy perfume.'
— Benjamin Graham

'When most investors, including the pros, all agree on something, they're usually wrong.'
— Carl Icahn

'The difference between successful people and successful people is that successful people say no to almost everything.'
— Howard Marks

'If you are a long-term investor, buying shares in a good business is more important than valuation. If you are not a long-term investor, what are you doing investing in the stock market?'
— Terry Smith

www.ingramcontent.com/pod-product-compliance
Lightning Source LLC
Chambersburg PA
CBHW071914210526
45479CB00002B/420